Managing Your Future

An Educational Guide

Belal A. Kaifi

© Belal Kaifi (2011). *Managing Your Future: An Educational Guide.*

Cover Design by: Cagri Tanyar

© Kaifi, 2011

ISBN-10: 1-936237-03-2

ISBN-13: 978-1-936237-03-6

	Subject Code	Description
1:	EDU032000	Education: Leadership
2:	EDU046000	Education: Professional Development
3:	EDU036000	Education: Organizations & Institutions

Printed in the United States of America by ILEAD Academy, LLC. Davie, Florida.

International

ILEAD ACADEMY

Leadership Education and Associate Development Academy

DEDICATION

As life-long learners, this book is dedicated to
each and every student. Good luck on your
educational journey!

TABLE OF CONTENTS

FOREWORD

Belal Kaifi, the author of this work, told me a story with which I was familiar: After appearing as a guest on a local Afghan television program where he shared his own educational and career journey, he was inundated by calls and emails from students and families asking questions about which classes to take in high school, entrance exams, resumes, and choosing colleges. He spent time patiently returning these calls and emails, explaining to each correspondent the differences between community colleges and state colleges, the nuances of entrance exams, and the importance of accreditation when selecting an institution. His experience was familiar to me because this is a pastime of my own. I have, at times, helped family and friends choose their classes, develop their resumes, and apply to colleges. During these encounters, I have frequently wished that there was a resource I could give, perhaps a book, to people with such questions. When I met Belal, I was pleased to learn that he would, in fact, write that very book.

This book begins by teaching the reader the basic terminology and vocabulary of education and then moves on to illuminate the greater complexities of degrees, graduate school, entrance exams, and internships. However, in addition to the practical and immensely helpful contextual information in this work, the reader will be pleased to find a sub-context of *wisdom* embedded throughout this book. The reader of this work will discover a delightful compilation of sound advice, genuine anecdotes, and real-world examples from which to learn.

This appropriate balance of advice and modeling is what makes this book successful. While in earlier chapters, he encourages students to seek out appropriate *mentors,* in the final chapter, Belal offers a list of sage *unspoken* attributes of successful individuals who have achieved their educational and career goals. He provides specific and compelling personal stories of a diverse group of professionals in an array of fields who share their struggles with these very issues.

Finally, I hope that the reader will understand that Belal does not simply write these chapters for the sake of putting out empty advice and suggestions to students; in fact, he is an excellent example of someone *implementing* many of these suggestions.

In my discussions with Belal, he expressed a genuine and honest concern about the lack of guidance and leadership available for students, especially those from immigrant backgrounds, who are interested in advancing their education. In Chapter 9, Belal tells his readers to "develop an internal locus of control," and true to his words, he has been remarkably focused on his own goal to write and produce this text. Earlier in the book, Belal emphasizes the importance of *networking* to achieve one's goals, and his ability to secure the many colorful and instructive interviews shows his own ability to network and connect to others. My point is that the author of this work is personally vested and engaged with the ideas, concepts, and recommendations he provides for his readers. The result is not only an immensely helpful reference and resource guide, but also an inspirational model for thinking and learning.

~Dr. Marina Aminy

PREFACE

I would like to thank all of the students and professors over the years who have contributed to my book in so many different ways. This book is a result of five years of research and hundreds of interviews and conversations with professionals all over the world. It must be mentioned that this book is both subjective and objective and should be used as a guide while understanding that information changes rapidly and more importantly, expectations and regulations in education also change.

As a first generation Afghan-American, I can recall having educational questions that my parents could not answer. At times, I was perplexed and had to figure things out on my own. Interestingly enough, working in education has helped me realize that many students have the same questions that I once had about the educational journey. This book is a comprehensive guide that illuminates the educational journey starting from high school and moving all the way up to a post-doctoral program. Each phase of the educational journey is starkly different and each decision is crucially important.

This book provides useful advice, tips, and guidance from experts in the field who have spent many years mastering their vocations. The interviews in Chapter 8 with elite professionals (software engineer, professor, medical doctor, pharmacist, teacher, registered nurse, police officer, lawyer, human resource manager, civil engineer, global musician, and school counselor) are invaluable and serve as the foundation of this book. By reading this book, a person is exposed to information that can only broaden horizons.

~Belal A. Kaifi
Antioch, California, 2010

Acknowledgments

There are many individuals who have formally or informally contributed to this book and I am thankful for their generosity and friendship.

1. First, I would like to thank my family for their ongoing support.

2. Second, I would like to thank my colleagues (Dr. Bahaudin Mujtaba, Mr. James Anderson, Ms. Wajma Aslami, and Dr. Marina Aminy) for their contributions and guidance in preparing the content of this book.

3. Third, I thank you for reading this material.

"I am a citizen, not of Athens or Greece, but of the world."

~Socrates

"It must be remembered that the purpose of education is not to fill the minds of students with facts...... it is to teach them to think, and always to think for themselves."

~Robert Hutchins

"Success doesn't come to you...you go to it."

~Marva Collins

CHAPTER 1

Introduction

"If you can dream it, you can do it."
— Walt Disney

*E*ducation is a journey—a journey that starts you on the right path to the rest of your life. As a matter of fact, many believe that education is the key to success in the 21st century. The global workforce has blossomed into an educated group of individuals who have the knowledge and experience to compete for multiple positions. Therefore, acquiring a sound education is necessary in order to be able to compete in this global economy. Many are aware of the *brain drain policy* and the negative implications that are associated with it. Furthermore, organizations have become notorious for *outsourcing* work abroad to cut costs. A case in point is how technological advancements have allowed for digital images (x-rays) to be analyzed by medical doctors (radiologists) outside of the U.S. Consequently, with unemployment levels high, elite international professionals from developing nations being recruited by top U.S. organizations (brain drain), and U.S. jobs being sent abroad, a student in the U.S. is faced with many important decisions. From an economical perspective, with supply of skilled workers high and demand low, it is imperative for each person to be more competitive than the elite professionals who are being recruited from developing nations. This phenomenon indicates that individuals need more education; hence, exceptional quantitative and qualitative skills. This book is merely an attempt to prepare students for the long journey ahead and will provide practical advice that will assist each student in all of their endeavors as *life-long learners*.

Life-long Learning

The latest knowledge and successful practices of planning and implementing education for life-long learning suggest that life-long learning is more than just education and training beyond formal schooling. A life-long learning framework encompasses learning throughout the life cycle, from birth to grave and in different learning environments, formal, non-formal, and informal. According to Reich, "Life-long learning, beginning in early childhood and extending all the way through a person's career, has to become the norm for all our people" (2002, p. 65). Being able to embrace change and learn a new skill is extremely important, especially in this contemporary society which is precisely why life-long learning should become a norm. With technology being so powerful and efficient, many careers have become endangered. For example, bank tellers have been replaced by ATM machines. "The number of transactions completed via ATM has exploded in recent years. There were 3.5 million transactions by ATM in 1985; in 1995, there were 10 billion ATM transactions" (Tregarthen & Rittenberg, 2000, p. 249). As a matter of fact,

> Jobs in the old mass-production economy came in a few varieties (research, production, sales, clerical, managerial, professional), but this system has fragmented. Computers, the internet, and digital commerce have exploded the old job categories into a vast array of new niches, creating a kaleidoscope of ways to make a living (Reich, 2002, p. 71).

It is fair to say that times have changed, the future is unpredictable, and the sky is the limit for people seeking opportunities to grow and specialize in all careers. Finding *that right career* is the "million dollar question" which has been researched by many professionals and scholars. A personality test can be useful but may not be the optimum solution to this conundrum. Regardless of an individual's profession, he or she will be required to learn and acquire new skills. This means an individual must be able to adapt to new situations and get out of his or her comfort zone. Life-long learning requires, "an ability to learn on the job- to discover what needs to be known and to find and use it quickly" (Reich, 2002, p. 73). Organizations are always looking to hire someone who is well-rounded.

Reich explains that, "the sharper a person's skills, the higher the person's wages" (2002, p. 74). If a person is well-rounded and approachable, he or she will thrive in any organization or situation. For example, the person's peers will feel comfortable coming to him or her for advice. An individual's goal in an organization should be to have his or her peers and superiors depend upon him or her for guidance and answers. On the same note, an individual in an organization should avoid being dependent on his or her peers otherwise he or she will be trapped, also known as the *organizational dependency trap*.

The truth is that society has groomed each and every person into becoming life-long learners who compete against each other for that number one spot. This concept is known as social-Darwinism or *"survival of the fittest"* which is a well-documented phenomenon in sociology, economics, and politics. Thus, life-long learning is an integral part of society and education. The educational system in many societies has prepared (*institutionalized*) each individual to become a career oriented person.

Institutionalization

According to Webster's Dictionary, the term *institutionalize* means "a strong attachment to established institutions." Many sociologists use this word to describe the behavior of prisoners after serving a lengthy sentence because they are accustomed to being in an institution; they forget how to function in a free society. The same frame of thought can be used for the educational system that institutionalizes students to be more punctual, dependable, responsible, and prepares each individual for a career. There is a stark connection between school life and work life.

During elementary school, secondary school, and post-secondary school, many can recall starting class promptly at 8:00 in the morning, having lunch at noon, and being excused around 3:00 in the afternoon. There were no exceptions and students were expected to be in class everyday and on time. There was also a small fifteen minute break or "recess" before and after lunch and each student was given about thirty minutes for a lunch break. This routine is practiced for over thirteen years (from the start of kindergarten to the end of high school).

Once students graduate and start working, they are faced with similar schedules, expectations, rules, and regulations. The typical work week is Monday- Friday which is also the typical school week. Workers are usually expected to report to work promptly at 8:00 in the morning, have lunch at noon, and leave work at 5:00 in the afternoon. In school, a student reports to a teacher and at work, an employee reports to a manager. Both the teacher and manager are responsible for assessing the individual on a regular basis. In school, students are given a report card based upon their performance, and at work employees are given a performance evaluation or appraisal based upon their performance. At school, students are asked to work in groups, and at work employees are also asked to work in groups. Working in groups allows students to *synergize*, learn different perspectives, and become more accountable. Interestingly enough, *intergroup theory* suggests that "two types of groups exist—identity groups (based on race, ethnicity, family, gender, or age) and organization groups (based on common work tasks, work experiences, and position in the hierarchy)" (Wren, 1995, p. 174). Both groups mentioned above are prevalent in schools and in the workplace. Thus, it becomes apparent that the educational system prepares students both academically and professionally to enter the workforce by setting strenuous rules and regulations that will be expected of all individuals in their respected careers. Upon graduation, students are institutionalized and are able to handle the demanding "8am-5pm" work week.

Obtaining an education and being institutionalized does not automatically mean that a person is going to be the ideal employee. The point here is that education is a journey, which requires a person to be a life-long learner, who constantly adapts to different situations. It must be mentioned that many go through school and merely "get by" with doing the bare minimum. This mentality follows the individual to the workforce. Specifically, many students are procrastinators, and procrastination can only lead to disaster in the workplace. Researchers Burka and Yuen (1983) explain, "Many people who were able to get away with procrastination during their school years are disappointed when that strategy doesn't continue to work as well later on" (p. 15).

Dealing with Procrastination

Humans procrastinate in different settings such as in their academic life, professional life, or personal life. "Anyone—young or old, brilliant or average, unemployed or professionally successful—can be a procrastinator. Procrastination does not discriminate on the basis of race, creed, sex, or ethnic origin" (Burka & Yuen, 1983, p. 4). Some believe that procrastination is a way of not revealing weak areas that need to be developed. Procrastination is something that should be corrected because of the negative implications it has on an individual. "Many people compare the experience of procrastination to living on an emotional roller-coaster" (Burka & Yuen, 1983, p. 7). Those who procrastinate in life actually put more pressure on themselves and limit their options for a promising future. "The demands and responsibilities of adult life are much greater, and procrastination begins to feel more like a prison than a game" (Burka & Yuen, 1983, p. 15). Balancing schoolwork, extracurricular activities, and spending quality time with family and friends can be a challenge which is why it is imperative to prioritize one's time accordingly.

Some individuals procrastinate while others prioritize. Prioritizing can help an individual objectively decide and organize a schedule for specific tasks to be completed. As a matter of fact, many successful leaders prioritize work in order to be both effective and efficient. "Academic procrastination which can be named as reflection of daily postponement to school life is defined as to delay duties and responsibilities related to school, or to save them to the last minute" (Engin, Tras, & Aydogan, 2009, p. 624). In school, work should be done as soon as possible because there should be time to proofread, edit, and even revise. This process is mandatory for success in graduate school and in the workforce. If a person knows that he or she procrastinates, then he or she should start giving himself or herself due dates. Some even create "to-do" lists that are carried around and evaluated every couple of hours. This concept of being productive correlates with being successful and using one's valuable time efficiently. When a person is striving for excellence, every second counts, and acquiring sound *time-management skills* becomes a life-saver. Those who continue to graduate school will learn that time-management is as important as networking or getting good grades. Some would even rate time-management as more important.

Procrastination becomes a barrier when submitting an assignment or project that needs to be of high-quality. When turning in an assignment, many professors are able to recognize how much time a student has spent on each assignment and whether or not the student waited until the absolute last minute to complete the assignment based upon several factors such as: punctuation, syntax, grammar, use of references, creativity, and understanding of the course material. Those who spend more time editing, proofreading, and revising assignments usually submit work of higher-quality and are more likely to receive the higher grade or evaluation. The same is true when writing a personal statement when applying to a university or when going in for a job interview. One needs to stand out, be well-rounded, and consider their global competition.

Global Competition

With globalization, countries are interconnected implying that additional competition is on the rise. As developing nations attempt to become more modernized and industrialized, they also create a high demand for educated professionals. There is a large wage gap between those with a high school education compared to those with a college degree. With technological advancements, there is a wage premium for highly educated workers, which encourages people to acquire more education. Education is a luxury throughout the world. A case in point is how in Afghanistan only students from the upper-class are able to go to college because of widespread corruption throughout the country. A student can pay his or her way into college. The same phenomenon is true in other developing countries throughout the world. As a result, students are forced to find alternative means to obtain a college education. Some are able to obtain F-1 visas (student visas) and travel abroad for educational purposes. This avenue has helped many foreigners obtain the education they deserve and has helped universities capitalize on the high tuition fees for international students. On the flip side, international students have raised the bar in education and have made education a strategic investment.

With universities dealing with budget cuts, there will be a rise in international student enrollments. Research shows that about seven percent of students at most universities are international students. This number fluctuates depending on the economy. For example, when the economy is stagnating or diminishing, universities capitalize on the high tuition fees of international students by simply enrolling more international students. According to the Federal Student Aid website for international students with F-1 visas, "A community college may charge a yearly tuition of $2,000; a highly selective private university may charge a yearly tuition of $28,000." On average, most students spend five years as an undergraduate which equates to over $100,000 for an education as an international student in the U.S. and of course some continue to graduate school. This is a perfect example of *hyperinflation.*

International students who come to the U.S. for educational purposes are willing to sacrifice everything in order to obtain a college degree. These students will study 12 hours a day and will compete for that number one chair. Competition is an understatement when evaluating the drive of international students. Most people would concur with their competitive nature because of all the high tuition fees they are forced to pay. International students with F-1 visas are only able to stay in the U.S. as long as they are full-time students. They must prove themselves academically so that they are recruited by a U.S. organization after graduation, otherwise they will have to return to their native country. A profit-maximizing firm will hire additional units of labor based upon the *marginal decision rule:* "If the extra output that is produced by hiring one more unit of labor adds more to total revenue than it adds to total cost, the firm will increase profit by increasing its use of labor" (Tregarthen & Rittenberg, 2000, p. 244). International students are known for majoring in computer science, engineering, and other technical programs that are currently in high demand in the U.S.

Supply and Demand

The rule of *supply and demand* is a construct from the field of economics but is relevant to all aspects of life. Those who understand the rules of supply and demand are able to make sound and logical decisions about the different choices people are exposed to on a daily basis. For example, in regards to gas prices, if supply is low and demand is high, then gas prices will increase significantly, and if supply is high and demand is low, then gas prices will decrease significantly. Therefore, the optimum time to purchase an 8-cylynder gas guzzler automobile would be when demand for gas is low and the supply of gas is high—because gas prices would be more affordable. From a different perspective, if there are a number of students (high supply) who apply to a specific university with a limited amount of seats available (low demand); then the supply and demand rules would yield a competitive enrollment rate that minimizes the chances of a potential student being enrolled. The same is true (competition) for employees in the workforce who are competing for promotions and raises and are viewed by employers as human capital.

Human capital is the set of skills a worker has as a result of education, training, and experience that can be used in production which is why recruiters ask for resumes that highlight education, experience, and training. It is important to have a significant amount of education, experience, and training in this competitive society in order to stand out from the rest of the competition because demand (number of jobs) is currently low and supply (number of applicants) is currently very high. The importance of doing research, being proactive, and figuring out what skills are in demand must be emphasized because of this highly volatile global society. An example is how accounting services are being outsourced due to technology, which means that the demand for accountants has decreased. Furthermore, the "dot-com bubble" during the late 90's was a time when there was a high demand for many professionals who were computer savvy. During that period, employment levels sky-rocketed and many college students decided to major in Computer Science (CS) or Computer Information Systems (CIS) because of the high demand and the low supply of qualified workers. As a matter of fact, at some universities the CS and CIS programs became "impacted" and students were waitlisted. Many of the students who graduated with a CS or CIS degree after 2002 were disappointed to find out that the "dot-com bubble" busted and more importantly, no one was hiring. The moral of this story is to spend time researching economical trends because there are jobs out there that are in high demand and that will stay in demand because of continuous technological advancements, globalization, and the demand for highly-skilled professionals who are willing to work abroad.

A field that is always thriving is the healthcare industry. The cliché, "there will always be sick people," is accurate and the demand for skilled health professionals is currently on the rise, especially with the new health care reform bill that brings down health care costs for American families. Some of the careers that are in high demand are: nuclear medicine technologists, registered nurses, diagnostic medical sonographers, and radiation therapists. Interestingly enough, there is currently a high demand for computer programmers because society is becoming more dependent on technology. If an individual would like to learn more about computer programming, then he or she should visit www.alice.org which is a free educational software that teaches students computer programming in a 3D environment. There is also a high demand both nationally and internationally for business professors. One report concluded that in the U.S. alone there will be a shortage of approximately 2,500 Business PhDs by 2012. The economy continuously fluctuates, which requires each individual to improvise, continuously learn, and be creative.

Creativity

Being creative is a talent that can help an individual throughout life because of its importance and relevance in educational settings, the workforce, and society. "Sometimes a problem requires coming up with entirely new ways of looking at the problem or unusual; inventive solutions. This kind of thinking is called *creativity*: solving problems by combining ideas or behaviors in new ways" (Ciccarelli & Meyer, 2006, p. 304). Being creative means to challenge the status quo by developing new and abstract ideas or methods. It is important to be able to think outside of the box and figure out new ways of getting things done which requires using imagination. Employers are always looking for *innovative* individuals who can help an organization develop new competitive advantages. In the academic world, being innovative is important when conducting research because of its real-world applications.

Those who are creative usually stand out in a crowd because of their ability to shine. It is no myth that universities and employers look for creativity in interviews and personal statements. At times, being creative also means being persistent and even aggressive in the job hunt process. An example is how a small percentage of people send their resumes to potential employers even when there is not an immediate opening, followed by an email to the hiring manager to schedule an *informational meeting* to discuss future employment possibilities. When comparing this creative strategy to the conventional method of waiting for an opening and then sending a resume to the human resources department (which may never be sent to the hiring manager) illuminates the importance of being creative, persistent, proactive, and aggressive in all aspects of life. Being creative also means accepting rejection and being able to find new ways of being marketable.

When being creative, an individual is able to discover many shortcuts. For example, students in doctoral programs are required to write long papers for each course and must also complete a lengthy dissertation at the end of their program that is defended in front of a panel. Many students who are creative quickly realize that all of the papers that are assigned in each course should be directly related to the final dissertation, and when it's time to submit the dissertation proposal, a student will already have several of the sections completed which will save a student both time and money (more of these strategies will be discussed throughout the book). It is important to be creative when choosing a major, a career, and a lifestyle because those who stand out will be successful. There are many examples of individuals who were able to think outside of the box when finding the right career. One professional, who received her master's degree in nutritional science, decided to take the registered dietician (R.D.) exam which she passed with flying colors. As a registered dietician, she realized that she is more marketable and knowledgeable but is still competing with many other professionals who have the same exact credentials. As a result, she decided to go to culinary school and become a chef who could prepare healthy meals for athletes. Her creativity and ability to think strategically will help her become a millionaire. A different professional who graduated with a master's degree in counseling with a special credential in marriage and family therapy decided that she wanted to stand out from her peers. She continued with her education and received a law degree that complimented her prior education and allowed her to become an elite divorce lawyer. Currently, there is also a high demand for individuals with doctorates in education who also have law degrees. This dynamic combination will allow an individual to be an educational lawyer, one of high demand and low supply. It is important to have the right experience, education, and training in order to stand out, and those with natural leadership skills are that much more in demand.

Be a leader, not a follower

Some people are more naturally endowed for leadership than others. The good news is that research shows that most people can be developed into strong servant leaders. Servant leadership emphasizes that leaders should be attentive to the concerns of their followers and empathize with them; they should take care of them and nurture them (Northouse, 2004, p. 309). Being able to deliver a warm style of leadership and paying attention to others are key elements of gaining the trust and respect of one's peers. The importance of paying attention is to show people that an individual cares, and the best way to do this is to pay attention to what they are doing, how they are feeling, who they are, and what they like and dislike. "Paying attention demands that you put others first" (Kouzes & Posner, 2003, p. 79).

Leadership is about behavior first and skills second. It all comes back to promoting positive expectations and having these expectations realized. A servant leader should always be in a positive mood, even though he or she may be overwhelmed with work, meetings, and interviews. A servant leader should always be willing to take a few minutes out of a busy schedule to sit down and listen to any issues a colleague may have.

Servant leaders are always complimenting and motivating their peers and recognizing their achievements. From this outgoing and friendly behavior, it is very easy for colleagues to open up and communicate how they feel about specific situations. Servant leaders will respect everyone's opinion, even if someone challenges an organizational policy. "Learning to understand and see things from another's perspective is absolutely crucial to building trusting relations and to career success" (Kouzes & Posner, 2003, p. 79). Servant leaders treat people better than they would like to be treated. "You express joy in seeing others succeed, you cheer others along, and you offer supportive coaching, rather than being a militant authority figure who is out patrolling the neighborhood" (Kouzes & Posner, 2003, p. 77).

Servant leaders are followed because people trust and respect them, rather than the skills they possess. Leadership is both similar and different from management. Management relies more on planning, organizing, and controlling. Leadership relies on some management skills too, but more so on qualities such as integrity, honesty, humility, courage, commitment, sincerity, passion, confidence, wisdom, determination, compassion, and sensitivity. It is important to understand that "as you take the role of a caring leader; people soon begin relating to you differently" (Kouzes & Posner, 2003, p. 77).

The 10,000 Hour Rule

Many people do not know about the "ten thousand hour rule" and its relevance to becoming successful. The ten thousand hour rule is a concept that has been proven to be accurate time after time. The rule emphasizes the amount of time that is needed in a specific field to acquire a set of skills that can be recognized on an international level. In the early 1990s, a psychologist by the name of Dr. K. Anders Ericsson conducted a study and concluded that ten thousand hours of practice is required to achieve the level of mastery associated with being a world-class expert—in anything. Thus, ten thousand hours is the magic number of greatness.

Many researchers have interviewed successful professionals (basketball players, soccer players, and chess players) and have determined in all cases that the same amount of time has been invested to reach such high levels. A case in point is Dr. Bill Joy, the *computer programmer* who "co-founded the Silicon Valley firm Sun Microsystems, which was one of the most critical players in the computer revolution. There he rewrote another computer language—Java—and his legend grew still further" (Gladwell, 2008, p. 37). Many compare him to Bill Gates of Microsoft. Dr. Bill Joy explained that he also spent about ten thousand hours programming. Many believe that certain people are gifted with talents that have helped them master specific fields. Research shows that practice and dedication are key factors to success as opposed to natural talent. For example, most people consider Mozart to be a genius, "the greatest musical prodigy of all time—couldn't hit his stride until he had his ten thousand hours in" (Gladwell, 2008, p. 42).

At the earliest stage possible, it is important for parents to introduce kids to tangible objects such as: a soccer ball, a violin, or a chess board in order to allow sufficient time for a kid to develop a passion for a skill that they will be able to master on an international level. An Afghan-American prodigy by the name of Salar Nader (born June 20th 1981) has astonished the musical industry with his "*tabla*" (percussion instrument) playing skills that are not only impressive but also brilliant. His father purchased his first pair of tablas for him when he was only six months old and by the time he was three years old, he was already playing at family gatherings. By the time he was in his early teens, he was performing with international musicians. Currently, Salar has been traveling and performing internationally and is known as Afghanistan's elite musician. Growing up, Salar spent a myriad amount of time practicing and perfecting his "golden touch" which he is recognized for, and will one day approach the ten thousand hours mark becoming *Ustad* Salar Nader. In the context of eastern classical music, the title "Ustad" is a distinguished and honorary title given to a person who has mastered a musical skill.

Being able to reach ten thousand hours is not an easy task. "It's all but impossible to reach that number all by yourself by the time you're a young adult. You have to have parents who encourage and support you" (Gladwell, 2008, p. 42). Parents play a tremendous role by first introducing a child to a new domain and then supporting and celebrating each milestone that can eventually flourish into a specific life-long skill that is appreciated and recognized on an international level.

Obtaining an Education

The 21st century is full of obstacles, competition, and choices. Students will have to make important choices that will have an impact on their entire life. A student's biggest decision will be how to manage his or her future by obtaining a sound education. Some will decide to start off at a community college or a vocational college; others may start an online program, while others move out and go to a traditional four year university. As mentioned above, there are many potential avenues to take, but the question is what is the most feasible? This book will address many of the options available to students and specific shortcuts that will assist each individual with finding the right career path. Individuals do not have time to waste because time is precious and valuable.

The better one knows himself or herself, the more successful he or she will be in college. Each person knows his or her strengths and weaknesses, which can be helpful when figuring out a major to study. Some people are more quantitative oriented while others are more qualitative oriented. For example, if a person likes numbers (quantitative) and solving equations, then he or she would probably be interested in the science or engineering fields. There are different learning styles (VARK): visual, audio, reading/writing, and kinesthetic that can also play a role in choosing a major. Students should know their learning style and how they will use their learning style to their benefit. There has been much research on the right and left side of the brain. Those who rely more on the right side of their brain are more creative while those who rely more on the left side of their brain depend more upon facts.

Many career counselors also recommend using different assessments to understand a personality that is consistent with specific majors and careers. One of the most popular personality tests is the Meyers-Briggs Type Indicator that results in scores on four dimensions of personality. Each person has a unique outcome that can help delineate why a person scored a specific way. Also, a different assessment is the leadership task vs. relationship orientation survey that produces a leadership orientation preference. There are many other assessments that can be used to help individuals figure out where they will be most successful. This book is intended to help guide students in the right direction by offering strategies, tips, and advice.

The following chapters will address topics related to high school education, undergraduate education, graduate education, post-graduate education, online education, vocational education, and the importance of networking and mentoring. Furthermore, conversations with professionals in different fields will be included to help illustrate experiences, shortcuts, advice, and lessons learned that will assist students on their important journey. Their advice may be able to save a student both time and money. The following chart represents the lifetime income of an individual based upon his or her education level.

Figure 1 - Lifetime Income by Education

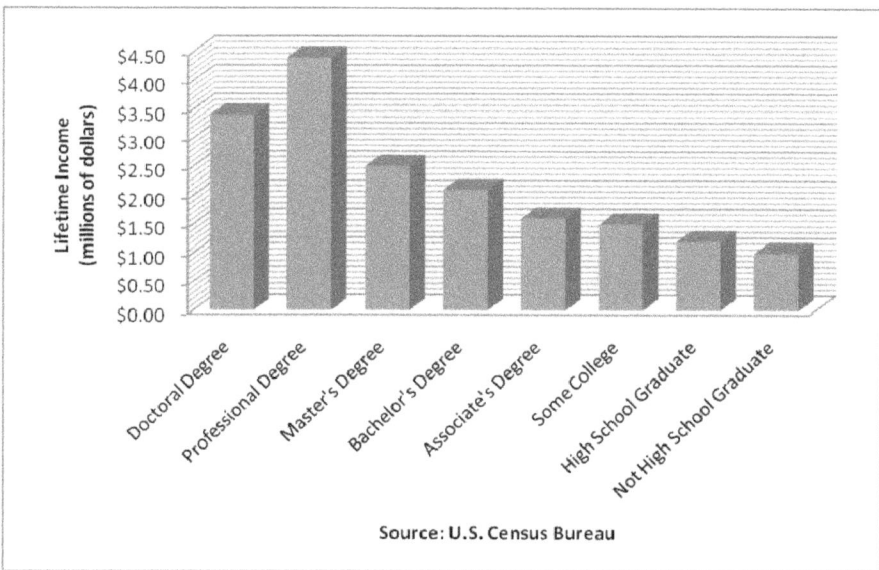

Source: U.S. Census Bureau

Summary

This chapter described some of the realities of the 21st century. Those with higher levels of education usually end up having more opportunities in life. Being prepared for an educational journey requires planning and discipline.

Chapter One Discussion Questions

1. Why do so many students procrastinate? How can procrastination eliminate opportunities?
2. How has globalization impacted you and your family?
3. Why is it important to be able to think outside of the box (be creative) in all aspects of life?
4. Why should you be a leader? How will being a leader help you in the long-run?
5. How will you implement the "10,000 hour rule" in your life?

CHAPTER 2

High School Education

"Make sure you have your priorities straight."

*H*igh school years are unforgettable for many reasons and each person has different recollections of his or her experiences. Many would agree that high school prepares individuals for the "real world" because of the competition in academics, sports, popularity, social clubs, and extracurricular activities. For the first time, students are exposed to the concept of *social-Darwinism*. Some students in high school work endlessly to obtain an academic or athletic scholarship, so that they can get into a top university while others focus on the surreal high school experience. Throughout high school, an individual is ranked academically against his or her peers, often based upon each individual's GPA (Grade Point Average). A student is expected to have a high GPA, play sports, be involved in extracurricular activities, and participate in social clubs, all while going through the process of cognitive development, physical development, and puberty. This phenomenon has been researched by many psychologists (Erikson, Freud, Harlow, and Piaget). The years spent in high school are truly convoluted for teenagers because of all of the different factors that influence their abilities to focus on school and only school. More importantly, being successful in high school will most likely equate to being successful in college and in the real world. This chapter will focus on the importance of high school and how high school can be used strategically to open up more doors throughout one's life.

There are many important factors that should be taken into consideration when a student is in high school and preparing for college. When applying to a university, the first step is for the admissions team to review the student's high school GPA, scores on the SAT (Scholastic Aptitude Test) and/or ACT (American College Test), and also the grades received in college preparatory courses, including AP (advanced placement) courses.

GPA

GPA is very important, and has the potential to open up many tangible and intangible opportunities, which is precisely why high school becomes so competitive. Most students in high school have an average IQ (intelligence quotient) level of about 100. Albert Einstein had an IQ of 150, and there are many people in this society who have an IQ of 190 or higher. As a matter of fact, IQs range from 0 to above 200 and among children to above 250. There are some students who are able to learn new and abstract material based upon their high IQ without much studying while others have to work strenuously to learn the same material. Like everything else in life (hair color, eye color, and height), IQ is hereditary to a certain extent. This does not mean that someone with a low IQ cannot be as successful as or even more successful than someone with a high IQ. As mentioned above, it is the time that is invested in a specific task that determines the level of success one will have. For example, a person with a lower IQ may have to work harder at learning new material but may actually learn more during the process. Those who will be successful in life should have both *analytical intelligence* (book smarts) and also *practical intelligence* (street smarts). Psychologist Robert Sternberg explains how practical intelligence is understanding what to say to whom, knowing when to say it, and knowing how to say it for maximum effect.

Colleges and universities seek students who have high GPA's because in their eyes, high GPA's reflect an ability to strive for excellence. There has been much controversy over the value of a high GPA when comparing different school districts with students from different socioeconomic backgrounds throughout the U.S. For example, is a 4.0 GPA in the Oakland Unified School District of California the same as a 4.0 GPA at Los Gatos- Saratoga Union High School District of California (which is ranked nationally according to *U.S. News & World Report*)? The point here is that each individual should be able to think and plan strategically by figuring out how to optimize his or her educational experience in this society. Interestingly enough, Frank Worrell, an educational psychology professor at UC Berkeley, explained "students with strong grades are more likely to succeed in college—but that a 4.0 GPA is by no means an absolute value" and further stated, "If you are in a school where the standards are lower, an A doesn't mean the same as it does in a school that's more rigorous" (2010, A19). A college student named Michelle recalled how she worked hard to maintain her high GPA and said,

> When my counselors or teachers would come across scholarships for those who are academically excelling, they would always make sure to let me know about them. I was awarded two different scholarships because of my GPA. Also, some of the schools to which I applied offered me an academic scholarship that was good for all four years of college, as long as I was never on academic probation while attending that college and that was simply based on my high school GPA.

The student above went to a high school where the majority of the students spoke English as a second language, which gave her a big advantage because she was able to understand and comprehend concepts much more quickly. She was awarded two different scholarships based upon her academic performance. A different student named Ronald shared his experiences in high school by stating,

> It was important to have a high GPA if one wanted to get into a four year college because the higher the GPA you had, the higher the chance you had to get in. Furthermore, with a higher GPA, it was more likely to get accepted with a lower SAT/ACT score. I wasn't a

very good test taker, especially when it was a timed test, so I knew that it was important to always keep my GPA high to have some leeway when it came to the SAT and the ACT.

The student above clearly used a strategy to figure out how he could optimize his chances of getting into a university by focusing on his grades. Research does show that a high GPA in high school will overshadow a lower than expected score on a standardized test at many universities (though not all). After reviewing grades, the admissions team reviews scores on the standardized SAT and/or ACT to determine how the student ranks amongst his or her peers on a larger scale (nationally), because an individual's GPA can at times, be based on subjectivity. An example is how one student explained how she was able to receive extra credit in a class which bumped up her grade from 89% (B+) to a 90% (A-) because she brought in donuts.

SAT/ACT

Taking the SAT or ACT is a crucial part of high school for those who are interested in attending a four year university. Most universities prefer the SAT scores over the ACT. Most educators agree that a student should spend about 100 hours studying and preparing for the SAT and ACT. The SAT score range is from 600 to 2,400. Thus, a perfect score on the SAT is a 2,400 on the three-part (math, reading comprehension, and writing) exam. Each section receives a score on the scale of 200–800. The average score (nationally) on the SAT is anywhere from 1,350 to 1,500. Interestingly enough, Harvard University has been known to reject student applicants who received perfect scores of 800 on the SAT math exam; Yale University has been known to reject student applicants who scored a perfect 2,400 on the three-part SAT; Princeton University turns away hundreds of high school applicants with 4.0 grade point averages. Many universities set their own minimum acceptance score that is located on the university's admissions website. Some universities also expect students to take the SAT II exam, which is an assessment that measures knowledge in a particular subject area such as physics, chemistry, or history.

The good news is that most universities set reasonable standards that can be met.

Most students take the PSAT (Preliminary SAT) in their sophomore year of high school and the actual SAT in their junior year of high school. The PSAT score is usually not sent to universities and is used as a benchmark for improvement. Performing well on the SAT is possible for each and every individual. Students have plenty of time to prepare for the exam and should start preparing their freshman year of high school. One student named Paul who scored above average explained,

> My parents bought me an SAT online program, and I used it way more than the practice book that I had because it was more interactive, kind of like a game. It was very useful and had learning techniques for the various types of learners. I studied every day after school until I felt comfortable to take the exam.

There are also many classes available for students who are seeking assistance with mastering the SAT. The exam is multiple choice and is timed. The time factor is what makes the exam difficult for most people. A student named James explained his strategy on the SAT,

> I am very thorough when I take exams, and I usually run out of time. I was advised that if I am running out of time on the SAT, I need to make educated guesses on the easier questions and skip the harder ones. This strategy helped me significantly.

Just like everything else in life, it is important to be proactive and learn as much about the SAT as possible. There are many useful books, websites, and informational resources available for those who need additional information. The one important concept to remember is that math, reading, and writing assessments are also used for graduate level entry exams and the earlier an individual learns to be a strategic test-taker, the more confident he or she will be when taking standardized exams. This means that a student needs to continuously develop his or her qualitative and quantitative skills in order to be successful and competitive.

AP and Honors Courses

With high school being so competitive, students are able to get ahead by planning strategically. The two most popular ways to get ahead in high school are by either taking AP (Advanced Placement) courses or Honors courses. Both have different implications and requirements. Students who want to earn college credits take AP courses in high school. "At the end of the school year, the students in AP courses take a complex exam, and if they pass, they will earn college credits," explained one high school counselor from Orinda, California. This strategy is very helpful and requires a student to spend a lot of outside time studying, reviewing, and preparing for the final AP exam. One student explained, "The AP courses that I took were equivalent to college courses. The AP test is a standard test and in order to pass the test a score of 3 or better (scale 1-5) is required and a lot of reading and studying outside of class." AP courses are great for students who want to graduate from college in the least amount of time and start graduate school. A student named John explained how he was able to pass his AP classes,

> My classmates and I would meet twice a week for two hours just to go over the material we discussed in class and material we weren't able to get to. Our number one goal was to pass the AP exam, which required a lot of reviewing. We also had to pay for the AP exam, and most of the class was taking it, so we were pretty serious about it because we didn't want to just waste our time and money for nothing.

Many students are able save time in college by passing their AP exams in high school, taking extra units during the summer at local community colleges, and planning ahead. A student named Joey explained the following,

Luckily, because I worked hard the previous years [freshman and sophomore], I was able to get out of school early because I had all my credits. I would get out early and work on my English Honors class and my two AP classes until my classmates were out, then we'd go to the library for an extra two hours, twice a week. The extra time we'd spend was good for us because my classmates and I would go over the material we read to make sure we all had a mutual understanding.

Students who take Honors courses take advanced level courses that allow students to boost up their GPA which helps when applying to universities. There are students who graduate from high school with a GPA higher than 4.0 because they take Honors courses. A high school counselor explained the following:

Honors classes require more time and dedication. The grades earned in Honors courses at most schools are given an extra grade point. With the standard four-point grading scale, A = 4 grade points, B = 3 grade points, C = 2 grade points, and so on. With the Honors scale, A = 5 points, B = 4 points, and C = 3 points. Therefore, when these grade points are averaged with a student's regular grades, the overall GPA could be higher than 4.0.

Those who are interested in getting into the best universities should consider taking many AP and Honors courses because the higher an individual's GPA is, the more competitive a student will be. It should be mentioned that it is not mandatory to take Honors or AP courses to get into a good college or university but it is highly recommended. As a matter of fact, Mike Kirst, professor emeritus of Education and Business Administration at Stanford University explained, "If you're not in AP classes, it's really quite dangerous" (2010, A19). The next step in reviewing an application includes evaluating a student's class rank, the application essay, and teacher recommendations.

Class Rank

In recent years, there has been much controversy over class rank and its relevance when applying to universities nationally. As a matter of fact, some high schools stopped ranking their students. The schools that still use this method to determine how students rank with their peers help universities figure out the overall ability of students to thrive in a competitive atmosphere. Competition, as mentioned above is something that is unavoidable and as individuals get older and step into the "real world" the competition only gets more rigorous. This is because the U.S. has an *individualistic culture* as opposed to a country like Japan who has a more *collective culture*. A current law student at Santa Clara University explained that "law school isn't so bad; it's the competition that is intolerable." Thus, many universities use the class rank as a method to filter out the students who are not as competitive when all other factors are the same. Interestingly enough, many question whether or not all factors will ever be the same in education. As mentioned above, is a 4.0 GPA in the Oakland Unified School District of California the same as a 4.0 GPA at Los Gatos- Saratoga Union High School District of California (which is ranked nationally according to *U.S. News & World Report*)? Is socio-economic status, being a minority, or being raised by a single parent taken into consideration when students apply to universities? Whatever happened to affirmative action to help minorities? Psychologist Beverly Tatum explains,

> Affirmative action can be defined as attempts to make progress toward actual, rather than hypothetical, equality of opportunity for those groups which are currently underrepresented in significant positions in society by explicitly taking into account the defining characteristics—sex or race, for example—that have been the basis for discrimination (1997, p. 117).

With affirmative action no longer being a part of the admissions acceptance equation, many believe that the competitive nature of high school does in fact benefit those who have higher grades and are ranked higher.

Some universities believe that class rank is more important than SAT scores because a student's class rank gives the admissions team an idea of how the student ranks among his or her peers in the same school, with the same teachers, and the same resources, which has fewer limitations than just focusing on national SAT scores. A high school counselor stated that "class rank is a much more accurate indicator of how well a student will do in college than SAT scores." If a student is ranked number one at a high school, he or she will have a good chance at becoming the class *valedictorian*, which is highly respected when applying to universities. A student explained how she became the class valedictorian. "I had perfect attendance all four years of high school, had the highest GPA in my class, was a tutor, and was the captain of the girl's varsity soccer team for two years." The class valedictorian is a true leader who leads by example. Striving to be the class valedictorian takes dedication, persistence, and vision which are all characteristics of successful leadership. Although class rank, GPA, and testing scores are important when applying to colleges, there are other factors that are taken into consideration. For example, a strong personal statement also has many benefits.

Personal Statement

At first glance, the personal statement seems like an easy task that can be taken care of a couple of days before the application is due. This mentality has proven to be incorrect and many regret not starting on the essay much earlier. What most people forget is that it is easy to write about others but can be difficult to write about oneself. For many universities, this essay tells the admissions team what a student's personality is like, what makes him or her unique, and how the student will compliment their university. A personal statement gives a potential student the opportunity to explain and justify certain areas of the application that are sub-optimal, but it is important to turn negatives into positives. For example, a student named Jose shared the following excerpt from his personal statement essay:

I am the first sibling in my family to obtain a college degree with all of the obstacles faced by my immigrant experiences. I started working at the age of fourteen and continued working throughout high school to help my parents with their finances. I can recall being in high school and waiting for the final bell to ring so I could rush to work. This experience helped me become more independent and resourceful and has helped me excel in every aspect of life. This experience has also contributed to my success in time management, entrepreneurship, and has taught me responsibility and accountability.

The person above is able to show that he is a hard-worker, is able to turn negatives into positives, and understands the importance of priorities. The personal statement is not a time to vent, complain, or whine about life experiences because everyone faces trials and obstacles.

Most universities pick the essay topic that the student will be writing about and so it becomes imperative for the student to use his or her creativity when addressing the topic. Students should be able to indicate what their overall objective is and what they will be doing with a specific degree upon graduation. It is important to keep in mind that thousands of other students will be applying to the same university and each student should be able to differentiate himself or herself from other applicants in a limiting two or three pages. When writing an essay, many recommend brainstorming with parents and peers, then preparing an outline, and finally working on the essay. The sooner a student starts on the essay, the more time he or she will have for others to proof-read and evaluate each draft. A student named Teresa explained her process,

Once my first draft was complete, I had my classmate who excelled in English proofread my essay. After I made the changes she requested, I had my favorite teacher read my essay. After I made her changes, I finally had my English instructor read my essay. This process took a lot of time but was well worth it. Each person who evaluated my essay was able to give me pointers on how I could improve each draft. I was very proud of my final draft and felt that it portrayed a clear picture of who I am and why I deserve to be a student at the university I was applying to.

As a student, it is important to have several people analyze the essay because others will be able to enhance the essay based upon their feedback and suggestions. Also, many counselors and teachers recommend that a student use a thesaurus when writing a personal statement. Teachers should be involved in the application process by reading and evaluating drafts of the personal statement and writing letters of recommendation.

Letters of Recommendation

Most universities require that students submit three letters of recommendation with their application because they give a student credibility, confirm a student's academic performance, and are written by professionals who are able to validate that a student will be successful. For some, getting a letter of recommendation is very difficult (they may lack practical intelligence) because they do not feel comfortable asking a teacher to write a letter for them even though they have the highest grade in the class. This mindset should be changed (*paradigm shift*) because teachers and counselors are expected to write letters for students who are applying to college. Also, it should be mentioned that teachers were required to get letters of recommendation when they applied to go to a university, again in their credential programs, and lastly by their employer when they were being interviewed and so they know the process very well and the importance of obtaining letters of recommendation. This phenomenon is not new and will always be significant throughout a student's educational and professional career.

When asking for letters of recommendation, it should be emphasized that students must ask someone who knows their strengths and who can write a strong letter of recommendation that will validate their abilities. When applying to a university, the admissions team prefers letters from high school counselors, teachers, coaches, and principals. The reality of it is that some teachers use templates when they write letters for students that they do not know very well. For example, one high school teacher explained the following,

> If I don't really know a student, I have a template that I use and I just add the student's name to it. If I happen to know the student, I ask them to write a two page synopsis of their goals, strengths, and aspirations. I use their synopsis as a guide when I am writing their letter of recommendation.

A strategy that is becoming more prevalent by students is asking all of their teachers and counselors to write a letter of recommendation and then choosing the top three letters that would complement the overall application. A different strategy for the students who know exactly what they will be majoring in is to have teachers from the same department write letters of recommendation. For example, if a student is planning on majoring in a science related field in college, it would be a wise idea to have three strong letters of recommendation from the student's high school biology teacher, chemistry teacher, and physics teacher, or if a student is planning on majoring in mathematics in college, it would make sense to have three letters of recommendation that are from a student's high school algebra teacher, pre-calculus teacher, and calculus teacher. It is important to get several copies of each letter of recommendation. Most professionals recommend briefing the individual who will be writing the letter of recommendation. A student named Josephine stated the following,

> When it came time to apply to colleges, many of my teachers were more than willing to write me a letter of recommendation because I always did well. My counselors were always very helpful because they were able to see that I was serious about school based on the grades I was getting in my classes.

If teachers recognize a student's abilities and strengths, they will gladly write a letter of recommendation that will increase the student's chances of getting into the university of his or her choice.

Students should send a thank you card or email to all of their teachers who took time out of their busy schedule to write a letter of recommendation. The final step in reviewing a student's application includes nonacademic and personal factors.

Sports and School Clubs

Playing sports in high school is recommended by many athletes, adults, professionals, and colleges throughout the U.S. Those who are able to play sports engage in a competitive environment where teamwork is rewarded, leadership emerges, and confidence is built. The memories last a life time and more importantly, playing sports in high school makes a student more competitive when he or she is applying to different universities. If a student really excels in a sport, there are also opportunities to receive athletic scholarships by universities who recruit top athletes. Most high schools have three different categories for those who are playing sports: freshman, junior varsity, and varsity. There have been freshman who have played on the varsity squad which is usually comprised of juniors and seniors in high school. One freshman named Adam who played varsity soccer explained the following:

> I started playing soccer at the age of six. My number one priority growing up was to become a professional soccer player. When I tried out for the soccer team my freshman year of high school, the captain of the varsity team noticed my skills and recommended to the varsity coach that I play with the varsity team. This was an honor because I was the only freshman selected to play on the varsity team. I played on the varsity team all fours years of high school which helped me get into a better university.

A college's admissions team looks for well-rounded individuals who are smart, athletic, and are natural leaders. A different student by the name of Eric explained how he was the captain of the school golf team,

I enjoyed playing golf and helping others with their golf game. I was selected to become the captain of the team which gave me authority and allowed me to lead by example. I was later given the MVP award. The combination of being the captain of the varsity team and being awarded the most valuable player helped me tremendously when I was applying to colleges.

A different award that most high schools give out is the MIP award which is the most improved player. This award shows that an athlete was dedicated and improved significantly which is commendable and sought out by colleges who are looking for individuals who strive for excellence. A different nonacademic factor that may help an individual become more competitive is by joining a school club on campus such as the chess club, math club, science club, reading club, or the drama club. School clubs are a great way to meet new people (network), brainstorm ideas with peers who have the same interests, and learn new talents and skills. The last criteria that can potentially help a student get into the university of his or her choice is an individual's participation in extracurricular activities.

Extracurricular Activities

High school is a time of exploring and figuring out how to live a comfortable life with many responsibilities. Many students have a lot on their plate during high school years because they are juggling sports, projects, exams, and a versatile social life. Those who are successful are able to prioritize accordingly. When applying to colleges, it is imperative for each individual to be competitive (as mentioned above) which is why some students start gaining experience in their field by "job shadowing" at an early age. For example, a student once explained how she wanted to major in Human Resources Management, so she asked her uncle if he would allow her to shadow him in the Human Resources (HR) department for which he worked. Her uncle was granted permission by his superior to have his niece come in once a week and shadow him. This became a win-win situation because the student was exposed to the tasks that would be expected of her and she was able to help the department by filing paperwork. It is always important to remember that when a student is job shadowing, he or she will work for free (*pro-bono*) but will learn and gain experience. Furthermore, by having this experience, an admissions team will acknowledge that the student is sincere about his or her major and has done some research. Many students who are interested in the health field also spend time volunteering at hospitals, nursing homes, and retirement homes. This valuable amount of experience will help a student later in life, which will be discussed in Chapter 4.

Some students are able to find time in their busy schedules for community service. Many universities seek students who were able to find extra time for community service because it is a service that is provided pro-bono. A student by the name of Jamal explained how he spent a significant amount of hours performing community service by stating,

> I would go to the Food Bank of Contra Costa and Solano County to help prepare boxes of food for the needy. It was not an easy job because I would have to carry heavy boxes full of food but it made me happy to know that I was making a difference in my community by helping out each weekend. When I was applying to universities, my manager wrote me a letter of recommendation and stated that I worked a total of 500 hours. I strongly believe that my good intentions and hard work was what helped me get into college.

As a matter of fact, most university applications ask if the student has performed any type of community service. Those who have that experience will once again have an advantage.

The last criterion that may help a student out when applying to universities is tutoring. An example of this would be an Honors English student tutoring ESL (English as a second language) students before and after school pro-bono or a calculus student who tutors algebra students in the tutoring lab for free. Being a tutor is not an easy job and takes a lot of patience and creativity. Students who want to stand out in the application process should be able to prove that they are willing to help those in need or work for free to gain practical experience that will help them in the long run. Thus, high school is a world full of opportunities that can become reality. Those who have their priorities straight and have a game plan will be successful. There are different avenues that can be taken in high school that will help a student when applying to universities. Even with all of the advice in the world, high school still remains the most challenging time for many students because of the external social issues that interfere and create barriers. A student by the name of Michael shared the following,

> As I look back at my high school years, I see it as a total waste. High school is nothing more than a social scene and a popularity contest, nothing more and nothing less. If I knew what I know now, I wouldn't have gone to high school at all. I would have instead passed the G.E.D. [General Education Development] exam and gone straight to a junior college. Not only would I have been ahead in life, but I also believe my life would have been a lot less stressful.

There are new and promising programs for students who would like to complete their high school education online. For example, Kaplan High School is an online program that offers a free and self-paced online education for students grades 9–12 with flexible start dates.

Summary

This chapter focused on the importance of high school and how high school can be used strategically to open up more opportunities in academics or athletics. It is fair to say that those who are successful in high school will have more opportunities in college. It all comes down to having a strategic plan in high school that will yield positive results.

Chapter Two Discussion Questions

1. Why is high school so important?
2. What should your number one priority be in high school?
3. What classes will you take in high school?
4. What subjects are you interested in?
5. How will you use high school as a vehicle to continue with your education?
6. How will you ensure that a teacher writes you a positive letter of recommendation?
7. What are some ways to indicate to colleges that you are in fact a well-rounded applicant?

CHAPTER 3

Undergraduate Education

"What exactly is your end-goal?"

*W*ith high school out of the way, students are now ready for the challenges of college. Most freshmen in college are about 18 years of age, meaning they are legally adults in the eyes of the American society and have more rights, such as voting. Undergraduate education is the foundation of an education because students acquire skills and training in a field that will prepare them for their next strategic step. Also, college life is very different from high school life because the same types of nurturing of teachers are no longer there, friends move away to different colleges, and students are faced with a myriad of decisions. Furthermore, the subject matter a student decides to study as an undergraduate will have an impact on his or her career, graduate education, and quality of life. Deciding what to major in is the most critical decision that a student will ever have to make because a student is committing to a long and strenuous journey that will open up other doors and adventures. For example, once a student decides on a major, the next step is to figure out what colleges or universities offer the best program. Deciding what to major in is not an easy process, especially when parents may insist on making that decision for their children.

Power Distance Index

The power distance index derives from Psychologist Geert Hofstede's research that focuses on attitudes toward hierarchy and how much a particular culture values and respects authority. For many minorities, respect for authority, parents, and elders is absolutely mandatory because they come from high-power distance cultures. The U.S. is an example of a low-power distance culture (everyone is an equal) where as Afghanistan is a high-power distance culture. For example, if Afghan parents chose a major such as civil engineering for their teenage son or daughter, then the teenage son or daughter would feel obligated to major in civil engineering even though he or she may have different preferences. This phenomenon has haunted many minority professionals from high-power distance cultures that are stuck working an 8:00 am – 5:00 pm job, five days a week, 48 weeks a year, until they retire. One minority medical doctor explained his story,

> As soon as I graduated from high school, my parents decided that I was going to become a medical doctor. I was a first generation American and my parents made all of my decisions for me because in our culture, children are unable to challenge their parents. My parents did not know the process of becoming a medical doctor and really didn't care; they just knew that medical doctors were wealthy. As a result, I became a medical doctor and I hate my job. If it was up to me, I would have become a college professor.

The story above depicts the influence that culture has when decisions are made for individuals who do not challenge authority to a great extent. Interestingly enough, people who come from individualistic cultures (survival of the fittest mentality) are usually affiliated with low-power distance cultures and people who come from collective cultures (members of a long term group) are usually affiliated with high-power distance cultures. One Afghan student explained how her father pressured her to apply to medical school after she completed her undergraduate work and urged her brother to major in mechanical engineering. She went on to say that her brother was recently laid off from work due to the recession and blamed her father for making him study a major that is in low demand.

There is a possible explanation for why minorities expect their children to become medical doctors or civil engineers (which has become the norm in many Afghan-American communities). The first point that must be taken into consideration is that most minorities come from underdeveloped nations where medical doctors and engineers are in high demand. Thus, those who have training in medicine or engineering are considered the elite of the community. As a result, minorities may believe the same is true in the U.S. The second point is that most minorities from underdeveloped nations have limited education and are not exposed to the different professions that create a society. Lastly, it is important to understand that some minorities do not fully understand that the U.S. is the land of opportunity, and a lucrative businessman or woman can easily be more successful than a medical doctor or civil engineer because of capitalism. The point is that in the U.S., young adults should be making their own decisions about their major and shouldn't allow others to interfere with their dreams because they are the ones who will be going to work each morning, investing all of that time and money earning their degree(s), and research shows that individuals will be more successful at their jobs throughout life, if they are passionate about them. It must be mentioned that students and young adults should be open to *suggestions* by elders at all times throughout their life. Most people would probably not want to be seen by a medical doctor who hates his or her job. Now, it is important to think about all of the different majors that are available to students.

Different Majors

As mentioned above, choosing a major can be one of the most difficult decisions that a student will ever have to make. The good news is that a student can always change his or her major if, down the road, something else more preferable comes along. Of course, changing majors is not recommended because of the extra tuition and fees a student will be required to pay, the excess paperwork that needs to be filled out and approved, and the additional time that will be required. A student has a big decision to make that will impact his or her life. Researchers and counselors believe that students should consider the following questions when deciding on a major: What classes in high school did you enjoy the most and why? What classes didn't you take but wish you had? What are your favorite nonacademic activities? All students should consider two specific aspects of their decision about what college major to declare. First, students should choose a major because they want to pursue a career in that field; second, the student should be fascinated by the subject matter. College students must think of this decision as a strategic chess move that will bring them that much closer to their end-goal. For example, if a student's end-goal is to go to graduate school and eventually become a lawyer, then he or she has the luxury of going to a great university and majoring in a subject that is in low-demand, getting a high GPA in that major, and having sufficient time to prepare for the LSAT (law school admissions test), which will make him or her more competitive when applying to law schools. The point here is that it is recommended that students focus on their end-goal and work backwards to figure out how they can save time and money. Many successful students recommend writing goals down and revisiting them on a regular basis. The educational journey of two physicians illustrates this point. The first physician explained how she went to a top ranked university in the nation by choosing a major that no one else was really interested in (less competition). She was able to get very high grades, studied for the MCAT (medical college admissions test) while in school, and continued to a top ranked medical school. It took her four years to complete this process. The second physician explained how he went to a decent university because he majored in a difficult subject that was in high-demand. As a result, his grades were sub-optimal. After he graduated, he knew his grades were not competitive enough to get him into medical school and so he went back to school and received a master's degree which took another two years. After that, he spent a year studying and preparing for the MCAT. After eight years, he was finally admitted into a decent medical school.

There are many resources available for students who are trying to figure out what to major in such as mymajors.com, which is a software program that will evaluate grades and generate a list of college majors that a student may want to consider. Also, students can make a list of their strengths and weaknesses which will also help in deciding on majors. For example, if a student excels in mathematics he or she may want to consider an engineering field and if a student excels in writing and communicating, he or she may want to consider a field relating to journalism. Some people are naturally more quantitative oriented while others are more qualitative oriented. By determining one's strengths, a student will be able to figure out what major(s) he or she will be most successful in.

Many professionals and researchers suggest that a college major can be determined by what a student is passionate about. Many students choose majors that result in high-paying jobs but are unable to complete the coursework and are stuck with a low GPA. It is imperative to do research ahead of time by figuring out what possibilities and opportunities a student will have upon graduation. For example, a student may have a relative who is a project manager who could easily help the student get a job as long as he or she has a degree in project management, or a student's neighbor might be able to help a student get an internship at an outstanding investment banking firm. A college counselor may suggest that if a student has both quantitative and qualitative skills, enjoys working with people, and wants to be well-off, the student may want to consider majoring in Business Administration because of his or her characteristics. Many people would agree that in reality "it is not what you know but who you know."

Some of the college majors that a student can choose from are:

- Aerospace Science & Engineering
- African American & African Studies
- Agricultural & Environmental Education
- American Studies
- Animal Biology
- Animal Science
- Animal Science & Management
- Anthropology
- Applied Mathematics
- Applied Physics
- Art History
- Art Studio
- Asian American Studies
- Atmospheric Science
- Avian Sciences
- Biochemical Engineering
- Biochemistry & Molecular Biology
- Biological Sciences
- Biological Systems Engineering
- Biomedical Engineering
- Biotechnology
- Business Administration
- Cell Biology
- Chemical Engineering
- Chemical Engineering/Materials Science & Engineering
- Chemistry
- Chicana/Chicano Studies
- Chinese
- Civil Engineering
- Classical Civilization
- Clinical Nutrition
- Communication
- Community and Regional Development
- Comparative Literature
- Computer Engineering
- Computer Science
- Computer Science
- Design
- Dramatic Art
- East Asian Studies

- Ecological Management
- Economics
- Education
- Electrical Engineering
- Electronic Materials Engineering
- English
- Entomology
- Environmental Horticulture & Urban Forestry
- Environmental Policy Analysis & Planning
- Environmental Science & Management
- Environmental Toxicology
- Evolution, Ecology and Biodiversity
- Exercise Biology
- Fiber & Polymer Science
- Film Studies
- Food Science
- French
- Genetics
- Geology
- German
- History
- Human Development
- Hydrology
- International Agricultural Development
- International Relations
- Italian
- Japanese
- Landscape Architecture
- Leadership Studies
- Linguistics
- Managerial Economics
- Materials Science and Engineering
- Mathematical & Scientific Computation
- Mathematics
- Mechanical Engineering
- Mechanical Engineering/Materials Science & Engineering
- Medieval & Early Modern Studies
- Microbiology
- Middle East/South Asia Studies
- Music
- Native American Studies
- Natural Sciences
- Nature & Culture
- Neurobiology, Physiology & Behavior
- Nutrition Science
- Optical Science & Engineering
- Philosophy
- Physics
- Plant Biology
- Plant Sciences
- Political Science
- Political Science – Public Service
- Psychology
- Public Administration
- Religious Studies
- Russian
- Science and Technology Studies
- Sociology
- Sociology – Organizational Studies
- Spanish
- Statistics
- Technocultural Studies
- Textiles & Clothing
- Viticulture & Enology
- Wildlife, Fish & Conservation Biology
- Women's Studies

Many students, who find it difficult choosing a major, go to a community college after high school and complete their general education and then transfer to a four year university. The community college option has become very popular for many reasons that will be discussed in the following section.

Community Colleges

Community colleges are becoming more prevalent throughout the country. Many students use the community college option as a way to save money, stay closer to home, and *buy time* for deciding on a major. The reality is that students who go to a community college or straight to a university must first take their general education courses which give students the opportunity to explore different subjects in different departments: humanities, music, foreign language, anthropology, geography, and many other subjects. For many, general education courses help filter out majors and subjects that are of no interest, while for others it helps with narrowing down a major to study.

There are some differences between community colleges and universities. Generally speaking, the majority of instructors at community colleges have master's degrees, and at universities, the majority have doctorates. At universities, the professors are required to teach and conduct scholarly research and in community colleges, the focus is mainly on teaching. The highest level of education that can be completed at a community college is at an associate's level and at universities at a doctoral level. The community college atmosphere is calmer and less competitive. At community colleges and universities, class sizes are about the same and instructors usually do not take roll. Students range in age, and many adults are coming back to further or continue their education because, "By the fast-approaching turn of the century, over half of all available jobs will require a college education and over half of those studying for undergraduate degrees will be twenty-five or older" (Kegan, 1994, p. 271). One community college instructor explained the following:

> The majority of my students are older than I am. At first, it was uncomfortable but I have proved myself to them and they now respect me as their instructor and peer. Thankfully, I don't have to deal with behavior issues in my classroom.

Community colleges have implemented transfer agreement contracts for students who are interested in transferring to specific four-year universities that are usually very competitive to enter. In California, the actual contract is called a *Transfer Agreement Guarantee* (TAG). This agreement can be used for seven out of the nine UC campuses (UC Berkeley and UCLA do not currently have guarantee arrangements). Of course, there are specific guidelines that must be met in order for a student to transfer to a specific university. For example, a student must complete all prerequisites and have a minimum 3.1 GPA in order to be guaranteed admission into an Engineering department at UC Davis. Each campus and department has different requirements and it is highly recommended to schedule an appointment with a college counselor for further information. A student by the name of Teresa who took advantage of the TAG program stated the following:

> I was so excited to learn about the TAG contract because I wasn't able to get into the university of my choice straight out of high school. I ended up going to a community college which saved me a ton of money and then after completing the specific course work and keeping up my grades, I transferred to the university that rejected me two years earlier. I transferred in as a junior and look forward to graduating. The TAG is truly a life-saver because for once, students reap the benefits.

Signing the TAG contract also ensures that a student will be taking classes that will count toward their major as opposed to taking classes that are not transferable. If there is no TAG contract for the university to which a student is interested in transferring, the student should use the *Intersegmental General Education Transfer Curriculum* (IGETC). The IGETC is a series of courses that community college students can use to satisfy lower division general education requirements at many campuses. According to one website, "The Intersegmental General Education Transfer Curriculum [IGETC] will permit a student to transfer from a community college to a campus in either the California State University or the University of California system without the need, after transfer, to take additional lower-division, general education courses." Many students make the mistake of taking courses that simply fit their schedule without first checking to see if it is a transferable course because they assume it is transferable due to the fact that they are taking a college-level course. It is recommended to have several copies of the IGETC form to make sure that a student is always taking the right classes and not wasting their valuable time. As mentioned above, it is imperative for college students to visit their counselor every semester or quarter to ensure that they are taking the correct classes, are aware of deadlines for TAG contracts and other scholarships, and learn of any new updates that may have come up such as teaching assistant positions. Students should develop a professional relationship with their college counselor and should be able to count on them for academic assistance. One college student by the name of Victoria explained the following:

> I met with my college counselor and he wasn't really helpful. He was pessimistic and didn't understand my goals. I mentioned my counselor's name to some of my peers and they laughed and told me to switch to a different counselor. I ended up changing counselors and was happy that my new counselor was able to understand who I was, my goals, and inspirations. She was outstanding. She even gave me a list of instructors in my major to stay away from based upon the feedback of her past students.

The story above illuminates the importance of students finding the right college counselor. Sometimes, a student may have to meet two or three different counselors before he or she meets his or her perfect match. Students should find someone with whom they have something in common, so they feel more comfortable going to them for advice and guidance. A student's college counselor will also have information regarding financial aid for those who qualify. Many agree that all students should apply for financial aid to see if they qualify because as a college student, one has nothing to lose and a lot to gain. Also, there are other programs for students who need financial assistance to purchase books and materials. All of this information can be retrieved from a college counselor.

University Life

After high school, some students take time off and travel, others enroll at a local community college, and some go straight to a traditional university. Friends who were once inseparable have to come to terms with reality and remember that this society rewards the survival of the fittest mentality and every individual has to look out for his or her best interest. Those who go straight to a university are usually the ones who either want to move away and experience life on their own or those who know exactly where they want to go to school and what they want to major in. For example, one student explained how he got into an elite business school and decided not to waste any time because his goal was to become an investment banker. It must be mentioned that going to a university is a lot more expensive than going to a community college; in terms of tuition, school fees, external fees, and even parking permits. Those who go to a university usually have to move out and either find an apartment or live in the dorms, which is expensive. One student explained the dorm life as a "wild adventure with nonstop entertainment." Imagine 500 students living in one building, sharing several restrooms, and with limited supervision. For some, this equates to paradise while for others, this equates to torture. Once dorm life begins, students are on their own, and no one is there to clean up after them. A student by the name of Brian explained his story,

> At first, I was excited to move out on my own and have my own little dorm. After the first week, I realized how difficult it was to live on my own and how nice I once had it. At times, my roommate and I disagreed on how things could be done and there was nothing I could really do about it. I spent a lot of time outside of my dorm room.

The story above portrays a different side of what most people experience when living in the dorms. In some cases, living in the dorms is cheaper than going off and finding an apartment near campus because at most universities, when a student is living in the dorms, he or she can also enroll in a meal plan for a discounted rate. A student can live in a dorm and have three meals a day for the same price as a one-bedroom apartment near campus. Both options are available to students. The key point here is that a student needs to find a healthy environment where he or she can focus on his or her education. Also, it is imperative for students to keep their end-goal in perspective when they are making each and every decision. A student by the name of James recalled how he met a friend in his math class,

> I was in my math class and I happened to meet a guy named Jabbar who also lived in the dorms. We were both freshman and really didn't have too many friends. Jabbar and I became close friends and we would hang out together before and after class. I was lucky to have a friend like him because we had a lot in common. We would work out, play basketball, and study almost every day. What was even more interesting was that he was my first African-American friend, and I was his first Chinese-American friend. We had a lot of great stories to share with one another.

If one's goal is to become successful, then he or she needs to always have an end-goal in mind. This can be done by forming study groups with peers who have similar goals. By forming study groups, students are also networking and meeting new people who may be able to assist them in the future when they are looking for their first job. At most universities, a student must complete about 125 units in order to graduate. As an undergraduate, a student should find work in his or her major to gain practical experience while earning his or her degree. Students should complete their undergraduate education with the highest GPA possible if they are planning on continuing with their education. Most do not understand the importance of work experience when applying for a job because they are under the assumption that a degree alone will get them a job.

Work Experience

As mentioned above, work experience will always play a big role when applying for a job. This concept is overlooked by some who believe that a college degree from a well-known university will automatically land them a job. For example, a marketing consultant shared her story by stating:

I was always an over-achiever in life. I earned my college degree and continued with my education and received my master's degree. I was on a roll and continued with my education and received a doctoral degree and believed that I would easily get a job because of all of my education. Unfortunately, I found out the hard way that individuals with significantly less education who had work experience were more qualified than I was. As a result of not having any significant work experience, I finally obtained a clerical job in a big organization where I gradually worked my way up.

Needless to say, significant work experience is mandatory during college years. Many organizations seek interns who are interested in gaining work experience. Interns are individuals who work for free and focus on acquiring experience that will complement their college degree. If a student is studying marketing, it is imperative for the student to find a marketing internship. Furthermore, if a student job shadowed during high school for two years and if he or she interned for four years during college, upon graduation the student will have a total of six years of relevant work experience. This will not only help students gain experience to get a job but also has the potential to enhance one's resume and make one more competitive when applying to graduate school. An individual who has interned for an organization for several years has the opportunity to obtain a high quality letter of recommendation that can be very useful. Also, by interning, students are potentially getting their *"foot in the door"* of an organization and upon completion of their education they will have the upper-hand when applying for a job because they will already know the hiring managers. Managers prefer to hire within (*internal*) an organization before they look outside (*external*). One person by the name of Julie explained the benefits of interning and gaining practical experience while in college:

I was interning and learned so much about my future job. I was able to put the theory that I was learning in school to use. I was making the connections and thriving. After I graduated, my manager asked me if I was interested in a permanent position and offered me a job. While I was an intern, they noticed that I was passionate about my job and respected the fact that I was willing to work for free. You have to pay your dues in life because there is no shortcut.

It is important to mention that a student will have to take a proactive approach and locate potential organizations that hire interns while he or she is in college. Consider the following two resumes from two students who both graduated from the same high school. One student went to a top university in the U.S. while the other went to an average university in the U.S. In college, they both studied the same exact major and upon graduation, they both applied for the same position at the same organization. After reviewing Figure 2 and Figure 3, who would be the better applicant to hire?

Figure 2 - Student # 1 Resume

Resume
Student # 1

Objective: S*eeking employment as an HR Specialist*

Education
Top University (2011-2015)
Major: Business Administration with emphasis in
*   Human Resources Management (AACSB Accredited)*

Oak Grove High School (2007-2011)

Experience
Teacher assistant at Oak Grove High School (2009-2010)

References
Available upon request

Figure 3 - Student # 2 Resume

Resume
Student # 2

Objective: *A professional with five years of progressive HR experience seeking employment as an HR Specialist*

Education

Average University (2011-2015)
Major: Business Administration with emphasis in Human Resources Management (AACSB Accredited)

Oak Grove High School (2007-2011)

Experience

HR Generalist at BAK Industry (2012-2015)
HR Assistant at BAK Industry (2011-2012) Internship
Job Shadowed HR Director at WAJ Enterprise (2010-2011)
Teacher assistant at Oak Grove High School (2009-2010)

References
Available upon request

Most hiring managers would be inclined to hire Student # 2 based upon the two resumes because Student # 2 has progressive HR experience. A successful student should be able to obtain an internship and not allow it to interfere with his or her college grade point average.

GPA

An individual's grade point average in college is significant for many reasons. Those who are interested in continuing with their education will need a high GPA to get into a graduate program. Those who have a higher GPA increase their chances of being accepted into a graduate program. There are some who continue to graduate school right after college and others who apply after gaining work experience. Those who are interested in graduate school are expected to have a high GPA. The following chart illustrates the difference between a high, medium, and low GPA.

Table 1 - GPA Range

Range	Quantitative GPA
High GPA	3.5 or higher
Medium GPA	3.0 to 3.4
Low GPA	2.5 to 2.9

Universities use different quantitative formulas when reviewing applications of potential students. For example, one university uses an index score methodology for students who are interested in their MBA program. At that university, potential students must have a 1,200 index score or higher in order to even be considered for admissions. The index score is calculated by multiplying a GPA by 200 plus the GMAT score. If a person has an overall undergraduate GPA of 3.0 and a GMAT score of 600, he or she would have a 1,200 index score. The formula is:

$$\text{GPA} \times 200 + \text{GMAT score} = \textit{Index Score}$$

Each university and department has their own method of determining who is eligible for admissions. One admissions director explained the following:

> Years ago, we realized that our admissions team needed to develop a more objective way of selecting potential students. We implemented a rigorous formula that we use for students who are interested in our graduate programs. Our new formula has been successful and we have a 90% retention rate.

As seen in the formula above, the higher one's GPA is, the lower their GMAT score can be and vice versa. Some are better test takers while others perform better in school. Those who have higher GPA's will also have a *competitive advantage* (sets an individual apart by having an edge) when applying for employment because employers have been known to review college transcripts for additional information on candidates. An individual's transcript is his or her academic story. Employers believe that grades reflect an individual's ability to perform under stressful conditions which mirrors the workplace. A hiring manager stated the following:

> I believe that an individual's transcripts provide me with sufficient evidence on how the potential employee will perform at work. For example, if a person has a lot of A's or B's, he or she is someone who will be successful at work while someone who has a lot of D's or F's is someone who is most likely going to be less successful and accountable. This is how I feel based upon my experiences.

There are many incentives for striving for excellence and attempting to receive the highest grades possible because many end up going back to school to obtain a graduate level degree and many management positions require a graduate degree. A civil engineer stated the following:

> After being a civil engineer for over 20 years, I felt that I was qualified to be in management. When I spoke to my supervisor about it, he stated that I needed a graduate degree in order to be considered for a management position. I had been out of school for over 20 years and needed to go back. Fortunately, my undergraduate level grades were pretty good, and I was able to get into a graduate program.

A student's college years will have an impact on the rest of his or her life which is why it is important to stay focused and have an end-goal in mind at all times. Those who focus on academics will have higher grades and will be able to receive letters of recommendation from their professors.

Letters of Recommendation

Letters of recommendation are important to have because a student will never really know when he or she will need one. Therefore, it is important to have updated letters that can easily be accessed and retrieved. The letters that students received from their high school instructors should not be recycled for when they apply to graduate school because a student will be expected to submit current letters from professionals who can attest to the student's abilities, skills, and work ethic. Also, it is important to mention that letters from family members are looked down upon because they can be biased. Students in college that are giving their absolute best in every class will have the opportunity and confidence to ask their professors for letters of recommendation. A professor of economics explained the following,

> I am known to write letters for those students who have earned the privilege of getting a letter of recommendation from me. I can't and won't write a letter of recommendation for just anyone and everyone because that wouldn't be fair and my students are well aware of that. My letters are usually at least two pages long because I want to make sure that I address everything that is relevant.

Professors are known to be busy with teaching, researching, and other duties and so the student will have to be persistent and should follow up on their request. It is highly recommended for a student to have a conversation with his or her professor about the letter of recommendation and how it will be used. A student can ask their professor to write a letter of recommendation that is very specific or one that can be used for different situations. For example, if a student is applying to become a Fulbright scholar, he or she should make sure that each letter of recommendation is very specific, but if a student is applying to several jobs, the letters can be more general and can be recycled. A student by the name of Samantha who is very ambitious shared the following story,

> When I was in college, at the end of each semester, I would email all of my professors and ask them to write me a letter of recommendation. About half of them would agree to

write me a letter of recommendation and by the time I graduated, I had over 50 letters. Only some of them were meaningful and usable. The letters were very useful when I applied to graduate school and also when I applied to different jobs. Currently, I have a collection of letters of recommendation that I review for motivational purposes once every six months.

Unfortunately, most students will not ask for a letter of recommendation. As a student, it is important to be a leader and not a follower. For some, asking for a letter of recommendation is difficult because of being afraid of rejection. The strategy mentioned above by asking several professors for a letter of recommendation has worked for many students because some will gladly say yes and others will apologetically say no for a number of different reasons. The point is that students have the right to ask for a letter of recommendation because they are entitled a letter of recommendation as long as they have good attendance, the right attitude, and high grades. The professors who write students letters of recommendation are the ones with whom a student should keep in touch. A doctoral student by the name of Eugene mentioned the following,

> Just the other day, I emailed my business professor from college for advice. I asked for assistance with my resume and she was able to give me some good advice and even noticed a small typo. I am glad that she remembers me and is still willing to help me. I hope to be able to do the same for my students one day.

For some, their undergraduate years flew by quickly, just as their high school years did, therefore, it is wise for students to get the most out of their undergraduate experience.

Summary

This chapter focused on the importance of college. College is a great time for an individual to earn the highest grades possible, gain work experience, and network as much as possible. College life is definitely complex and humbling.

Chapter Three Discussion Questions

1. Why is it so important to start working in your field of study as early as possible?
2. How can you tactfully discuss your academic decisions with your parents to minimize conflicts?
3. What are some of the benefits to going to a community college?
4. Why is it important to network in college?
5. Why are letters of recommendation so important? What is a good plan for requesting a letter?

CHAPTER 4

Graduate Education

"Life is like a bicycle. To keep your balance you must keep moving."
—Albert Einstein

*I*n the past, those who were interested in graduate education were either over achievers or interested in higher level positions. However, today many believe that a prerequisite to living comfortably in the 21st century is having a graduate level degree. There is definitely a correlation between higher levels of education and higher living standards. With the competitive global economy, graduate education is becoming more prevalent and many individuals have multiple graduate degrees. Those who have graduate degrees acquire special skills that prepare them to perform specific tasks. For example, if an individual has a law degree (J.D.) and has passed all of the required exams, then he or she can practice law and represent those who are in need of legal representation. In order to practice law, an individual is usually required to have an undergraduate degree, must have completed an accredited law program, and must have successfully passed the bar exam. A bar examination can simply be defined as an examination to determine whether a candidate is qualified to practice law in a given jurisdiction. As with every graduate program, there are specific requirements that must be met in order to graduate. In the academic world, the most common graduate level project is a thesis, which consists of producing original research in a specific field. This chapter will illuminate the different entry level exams that must be taken for specific programs, accrediting bodies, and tips on being successful in graduate school. The following chart shows the correlation between levels of education and annual salaries from a national perspective.

Figure 4 - Annual Incomes by Educational Level

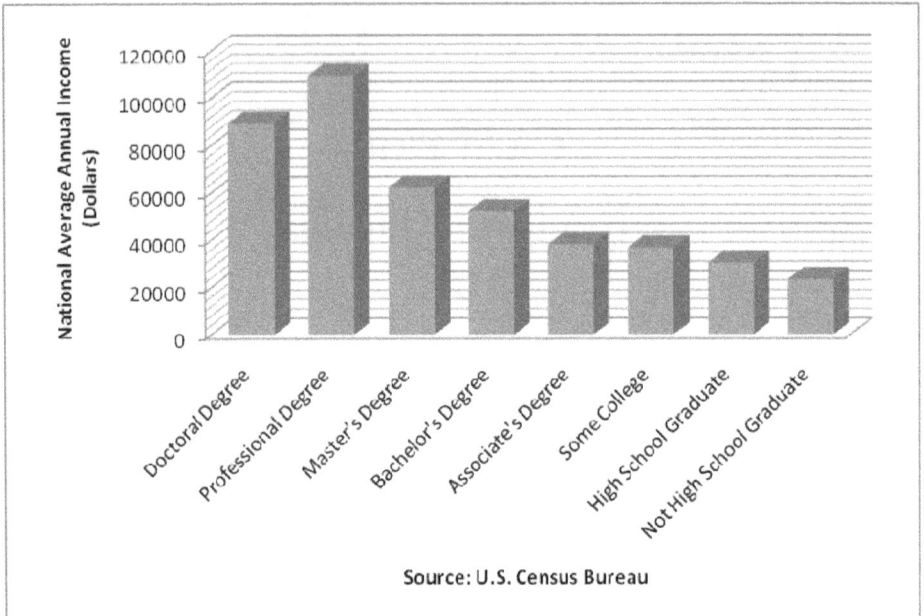

Source: U.S. Census Bureau

Graduate Level Entry Exams

When applying for graduate school, most programs require students to take an exam that is related to their field of study. For example, if a student is interested in law school, he or she is required to take the LSAT (Law School Admission Test), and if a student is interested in medical school, the requirement is to take the MCAT (Medical College Admission Test). A graduate level entry exam is used by universities as an indicator of how successful a student will be in a specific program when compared to his or her peers. Also, the results of graduate level entry exams are used for accreditation and reaccreditation purposes. The mean and median scores for each program can usually be found on a university's website and can be used as a benchmark. Graduate level entry exams play a significant role when admissions personnel make recommendations on who will be admitted; the assumption is that a graduate level entry exam is objective. Each university has their own method of evaluating student applications and have their own minimum requirements that are at times kept a secret from the general public. A college admissions representative expressed the following:

> When we make our decisions, we attempt to compare different applicants based upon many different factors. At our institution, we believe that the graduate level entry exam (LSAT) is more important than grades. Based upon our data, we see a correlation between high LSAT scores and successful completion of the Bar exam which allows an individual to practice law in a specific jurisdiction. Therefore, our data has assisted us in making sound decisions.

Each graduate level exam is unique and has different sections. There are many resources that offer useful information about each exam. The following chart represents the most popular graduate level exams:

Table 2 - Popular Graduate Level Exams

Program	Exam	Full Name of Exam
Business	GMAT	Graduate Management Admission Test
Sciences	GRE	Graduate Record Exam
Education	MAT/ GRE	Millers Analogy Test / Graduate Record Exam
Pharmacy	PCAT	Pharmacy College Admission Test
Law	LSAT	Law School Admission Test
Medical	MCAT	Medical College Admission Test
Social Sciences	GRE	Graduate Record Exam
Dental	DAT	Dental Admission Test

Preparing for a graduate level exam requires time, motivation, and a competitive drive because the final outcome will determine where a student will end up going to school. This means that a student's future is on the line and that a student will have to do everything in his or her power to ace the exam. A student by the name of Aaron explained how he studied for the GMAT,

> I was nervous about my exam but understood that I had to do my best. I studied for six months straight and then took a GMAT prep course to give me extra tips. I honestly studied seven days a week and at least five hours each day. I made sure that I took many practice exams and reviewed my test taking strategies. I ended up scoring in the 'above average' range which got me into a reputable business program.

Those who have test anxiety or are not great test takers must work twice as hard to master an exam. The more a student knows about an exam, the more prepared he or she will be to take the exam. Tutoring programs are also available for those who are in need of extra assistance. Many believe that it is imperative to research universities and the staff of each department prior to applying to a specific program.

Research the Faculty

As a student is preparing for graduate school, researching the university's history and reputation is part of that preparation, just as faculty members will be researching the student's file to see if he or she will be a good fit for their program. A student has the opportunity to research universities by figuring out what their strengths and weaknesses are based upon one's expectations. Considerations include who the faculty members are, what awards the faculty members have won, what and where they have published, and even how other students have evaluated each faculty member. A student should also consider the ratio of adjunct (temporary) faculty members to tenured faculty members. This is important because adjunct professors are paid significantly less and may not have the same type of permanence at the institution. Many believe that graduate education is very political because of competition and scarce resources.

A student must understand that undergraduate education is a time when a person is exposed to different theories and constructs relating to a specific field. If a student decides to continue to graduate school, he or she will be researching the same theories and will be expected to apply them to current situations. A doctoral program will give a student the opportunity to conduct original research and develop new theories. Historically, graduate education has focused on research and unfortunately, many universities have deviated from this reality which has restricted many students upon graduation. A student by the name of Alvin who graduated from a doctoral program explained the following,

> I wish my professors would have emphasized the importance of researching in my program. We spent so much time writing papers that were insignificant. As a result, I am learning on my own what I should have learned many years ago.

Students need to have the tools that are needed to be successful upon graduation, which means that a student with a doctoral level degree should be able to publish in academic journals. While in graduate school, a student should start publishing as much as possible. Students can publish in newspapers, magazines, books, and even academic journals. The more a student publishes, the more exposure he or she will have to the academic world. When students conduct research on faculty members, they can find out what their research interests are and where they have been publishing. If a student is able to find a professor who has similar interests and is actively publishing in academic journals, the student may want to have a conversation with this professor to see if he or she can help the student complete the program by spending the least amount of money, assisting the student in publishing in academic journals, and introducing the student to scholars in the field. Also, if a faculty member is interested in being a student's advisor, the student should make it clear that he or she is interested in publishing and would like to co-author research articles while in the program. A student can help by gathering data, proof-reading, editing, and by gathering relevant literature. If the professor is actively publishing, he or she will not have a problem with this request and if the professor is unwilling to meet this expectation, then the student may want to find a different advisor or even program. Although some universities are more research oriented, all professors are expected to research and publish on a regular basis. A researcher either "publishes or perishes" as one outstanding professor explained to a class of doctoral students. By the time a student graduates from a doctoral program, he or she should have numerous publications in order to compete in this global economy. A professor of finance explained,

> By the time my students graduate with a doctoral level degree, they will have at least five to ten different research publications in peer-reviewed academic journals, will have presented at several conferences, and will be fully capable of continuously publishing in top-tiered journals.

As a student researches potential schools, it is important to keep in mind that the student will be spending a lot of time with an advisor and that the student needs someone who is dependable, available, and credible. The last thing a student wants is to get into a program that will not prepare him or her for the real world where the individual will be required to teach, publish, and consult.

Pay Attention to Specific Accreditations

Many students have also learned that a program's accreditation is significantly important and should be researched ahead of time. Some student's believe that if a college or university is accredited, then all of the programs within the college or university are also accredited by the appropriate and most prestigious accrediting agencies, which is absolutely false. A student explained how she received a doctoral level degree in Business Administration and was unaware of the different accrediting institutions relating to business colleges and universities. She explained,

> I received a doctoral level degree in Business Administration from a well known university that was very expensive. When I was seeking employment, I found out that the majority of universities prefer a doctoral degree in Business Administration that is from an AACSB accredited program and my doctoral degree is from an ACBSP accredited program. I was flabbergasted and felt cheated. No one ever explained to me the different accrediting institutions for business majors. As a result, I am limited to where I can teach.

This student, like many others, realized (after the fact) that her four year doctoral program was not accredited by the highest business school accrediting institution which is the Association to Advance Collegiate Schools of Business (AACSB) and as a result is unable to teach in *some* of the top-tiered business programs that require that AACSB stamp of approval. The following job posting illustrates the importance of accreditation:

> Qualifications for the position include: (1) an earned doctorate in Business Administration from an AACSB accredited institution, with an emphasis in Management; (2) evidence of effective teaching; (3) evidence of a strong research agenda. Preference will be given to candidates with refereed publications in the field and presentations at national and international conferences. The College of Business Administration is fully accredited by AACSB.

The Association to Advance Collegiate Schools of Business (AACSB), International Assembly for Collegiate Business Education (IACBE), and Association of Collegiate Business Schools and Programs (ACBSP) are three examples of accrediting agencies for business schools and programs. Many believe that the "gold standard" is the AACSB accreditation for business schools. One university stated the following on their website:

> Undergraduate and graduate programs at the College of Business are accredited by AACSB. Less than 5% of business programs worldwide have earned this distinguished hallmark of excellence in business education. AACSB standards relate to curriculum, faculty resources, admissions, degree requirements, computer facilities, financial resources and intellectual climate.

The same is true for students interested in law school. The top law schools around the nation are ABA (American Bar Association) accredited. Those who have graduated from an ABA accredited law program will have more employment opportunities. Medical schools are accredited by the Association of American Medical Colleges (AAMC). This does not necessarily mean that someone who graduates from a non-ABA accredited law program or a non-AACSB accredited business program will be less successful. The point here is that students should be aware of the different accrediting institutions that relate to their subject matter and should make informed decisions. A student can easily check the status of each school by simply doing a quick search online or calling the school.

Master's Programs

Once a student has been admitted into a master's program, he or she will soon realize that there will be assignments, projects, and group presentations on a regular basis. Students become overwhelmed with their careers, ongoing homework assignments, and projects. Graduate students are pushed to their limits, and those who survive master the art of efficiency, improvisation, and efficacy. Most programs consist of approximately thirteen to fifteen courses, which can take approximately two years to complete. Also, classes are usually held in the evenings. Those who benefit the most from a master's program are the individuals who have practical work experience and can make connections from theory to practice (*praxis*). A student named Vanessa explained the following,

> I am working on my master's degree in school counseling at night and during the day I work as a substitute teacher. My experiences in the classroom during the day help me understand the concepts that I am exposed to at night. I would highly recommend for everyone to work in their respected fields during the day.

As you can imagine, being at work from 8am until 5pm, and then commuting to school and sitting in a classroom from 6pm to 9pm can be a daunting schedule to undertake. Some programs offer weekend courses as well to help accommodate working adults. Being successful in graduate school has a lot to do with time-management and being able to prioritize effectively. A student named Abraham explained his strategy:

> I would put together a to-do list every morning and would make sure that I completed all of my responsibilities before

I went to bed each night. My list was a life saver because I was able to strategically move forward with my work and complete most assignments ahead of time. This allowed for me to spend more time with my family.

Most working adults also have children, a social-life, and other obligations that must be taken into consideration as well. There have been many situations where relationships have ended, careers have been impacted, and families have been destroyed because of the demands of graduate school. Graduate students have been fired from their place of employment for focusing their time and efforts on their research projects as oppose to their daily tasks. Those who are planning on going to graduate school should first have a conversation with their family, spouse, in-laws, friends, children and anyone else that will be impacted by their busy schedule. Everyone should understand that graduate school is a big commitment that will last several years but will create more opportunities. By having this conversation ahead of time, those who matter will be more understanding. Being able to balance everything at once has been described by many as "the ultimate test" with many unforeseeable obstacles. Many professionals agree that it is important for students to be able to analyze their "use of time" throughout the day. The schedule in Table 3 can help students figure out when they have free time for extracurricular activities.

Table 3 - Weekly Schedule Example

	Monday	Tuesday	Wednesday	Thursday	Friday	Saturday	Sunday
7:00am							
8:00am							
9:00 am		Work		Work		Work	Work
10:00am	Class	Work	Class	Work	Class	Work	Work
11:00am	Class	Work	Class	Work	Class	Work	Work
12:00pm	Lunch	Lunch	Lunch	Lunch	Lunch	Lunch	Lunch
1:00 pm	Class	Work	Class	Work	Class	Work	Work
2:00 pm	Class	Work	Class	Work	Class	Work	Work
3:00 pm	Class	Work	Class	Work	Class	Work	Work
4:00 pm		Work		Work		Work	Work
5:00 pm		Work		Work		Work	Work
6:00 pm	Dinner	Dinner	Dinner	Dinner	Dinner	Dinner	Dinner
8:00 pm	Gym	Study	Gym	Study	Gym	Study	Family
9:00 pm	Gym	Study	Gym	Study	Gym	Study	Family
10:00pm	Read	Read	Read	Read	Read	Study	Family
11:00pm	Sleep	Sleep	Sleep	Sleep	Sleep	Sleep	Sleep

Aside from homework, presentations, and projects, students are also required to complete a master's thesis. A thesis is an original research study that explores a current issue in one's respected field. The thesis is anywhere from 40 to 100 pages long and is defended in front of a committee. A student usually selects who his or her thesis advisor will be along with other committee members. The process can be a long, frustrating, and humbling experience once the student is finished. A student by the name of Amber explained her experience,

> I was already overwhelmed with my classes, and then I had to start writing my thesis if I wanted to graduate on time. I spent numerous hours in the library searching for relevant research articles and books that I could use to support my ideas. I almost quit the program several times. Fortunately, I had the support of my peers who were there to assist me when I had questions.

Those who write a thesis and who continue to a doctoral program can use the majority of their work by transforming it into a doctoral dissertation which is a more comprehensive and detailed study. Some universities have also implemented a capstone course that can be taken in place of writing a thesis for those who will not continue into a doctoral program. At the end of the capstone course, students take a final exam that is a comprehensive assessment for the entire program and not just the capstone course. A student by the name of David stated the following,

> The capstone course proved to be very difficult. I had to read seven books in eight weeks and also review all of the material from all of my other courses. I wish I would have written a thesis because I spent the same amount of time studying, reading, and reviewing for this final exam.

Research has shown that those who complete a master's program will have more opportunities when compared to those who only have an undergraduate degree (Figure 4). For a student, it is important to be working in his or her field while completing his or her master's program because that experience is priceless. If a student is working on a MBA (Master of Business Administration) degree, he or she should be working in a business related field during the day. The more work experience an individual has, the easier it will be to get a promotion in that field because an individual's education will complement his or her work experience. While busy with school and work, a student must also start publishing. A sharp graduate student will publish book reviews in academic journals, write research articles with an advisor, and even publish in local newspapers and magazines. There are a myriad of ways to get published. Also, graduate students should subscribe to academic journals in their field. Having this exposure will allow students to be up-to-date with current trends in a field. Students usually receive large discounts when they subscribe to academic journals. By reading academic journals on a regular basis, students will have a better idea of what scholars in their field are researching and what conclusions they are determining that can help a student when working on assignments and projects. Those who do an outstanding job in their master's program and are interested in continuing with their education can apply to a doctoral program which is just as demanding and is another four or more years of commitment.

Doctoral Programs

Being admitted into a doctoral program is an accomplishment and finishing the requirements of a doctoral program is an even bigger accomplishment. Doctoral programs are meant for people who are interested in conducting research and teaching students at the undergraduate and graduate levels. There are many different doctoral level programs and degrees. For example, a person can get the traditional Doctor of Philosophy (Ph.D.) degree, a Doctor of Business Administration (D.B.A.) degree, a Doctor of Education (Ed.D.) degree, a Doctor of Judicial Science (S.J.D.) degree, a Doctor of Engineering (D.Eng.) degree, a Doctor of Psychology (Psy.D.) degree, a Doctor of Pharmacy (Pharm.D.) degree, a Medical Doctor (M.D.) degree, a Doctor of Osteopathic (D.O.) Medicine degree, a Doctor of Optometry (O.D.) degree, a Doctor of Nursing Practice (D.N.P.) degree, and other programs certainly exist. The "D" in each title signifies an expert who is considered a doctor in that specific field. All programs require dedication, motivation, and inspiration to be completed. An interested student can apply to a Ph.D. program in Business Administration or a D.B.A. program which is very similar because they are both doctorate level degrees in the field of Business Administration and are considered academically equivalent. A Ph.D. in Business Administration focuses more on developing new theories while a D.B.A. focuses more on the application of theory. As a matter of fact, many business departments have an even distribution of D.B.A.'s and Ph.D.'s who teach and conduct research. A job posting at a popular university stated, "Applicants must have an earned Doctorate (Ph.D. or D.B.A.) in Management or Entrepreneurship from an AACSB-accredited university." An assistant professor of Educational Leadership by the name of Ted explained the following,

> I was ready to apply to a doctoral program in education when I learned about the Ed.D. I spoke to my advisor on several occasions and came to the conclusion that the Ed.D. was what I was looking for because my goal was not to teach K-12 teachers but to become a school administrator. The Ed.D. program at our university was designed to help students acquire the tools needed to become educational leaders. I was happy to learn that many universities in America offer Ed.D. programs. The outcome has been priceless.

Advanced degrees are becoming more prevalent as specialized programs are becoming more popular. For example, a student can earn a doctorate in public administration (D.P.A.) if he or she is interested in managing a government affiliated organization. Doctoral programs are expensive and usually take about four to six years to complete. A student by the name of Barbara explained how she is struggling with her school loans,

> My undergraduate program cost me $15,000, my master's program cost me $20,000, and my doctoral degree cost me $65,000. As a result, I am in debt $100,000. The current state of the economy is not helping me out either because I am having troubles finding work in my field. This is not how I envisioned life after graduation to be.

Each year, the cost of education increases significantly, and many believe that education has become a business rather than a place of intellectual and professional growth. For example, many universities are starting to offer doctoral level programs to students who will not be able to teach or conduct research at an academic level.

Students in doctoral programs should be actively publishing in their fields. This point cannot be stressed enough because many students neglect the importance of publishing because they are so busy with their doctoral dissertation. As a result, students graduate with a doctoral degree but are unable to find teaching positions because of their lack of scholarly work. Many job postings state, *"Candidates must demonstrate an active research agenda, and have excellent teaching and communication skills"* or *"Evidence of teaching effectiveness is desired as is evidence of the potential to produce peer reviewed published research."* As many have realized, publishing in peer-reviewed academic journals takes time, patience, and determination. A doctoral student by the name of Sylvia explained the following,

> I wanted to publish as a doctoral student so I could impress my future employer as soon as I graduated. I sent in several articles and they were all rejected. I was very upset, and when I approached my advisor, she told me that was normal and to revise and resend the articles to different journals for publication consideration. The same thing happened over and over again.

Students become discouraged when their work is not published in academic journals. The key is to find the right journal that will complement the article. An outstanding peer reviewed academic journal for doctoral students to publish in is the *Journal of Business Studies Quarterly* (JBSQ) (www.jbsq.org). As mentioned above, students should subscribe to academic journals to learn more about publishing requirements, new trends in their field, and the etiquette of publishing in journals.

Those who are in a doctoral program should also consider teaching at the college level to gain experience. Instructors at the college level are expected to have at least a master's degree. Teaching experience and research publications will help significantly when applying for a teaching position at a larger university. There are many private colleges and community colleges who hire instructors on a term-by-term basis. Also, many universities hire adjunct (part-time) instructors to teach a course or two on a term-by-term basis. An instructor stated,

> I found work at the local community college. It was nice to be able to teach introductory psychology courses and also review the information that I had learned many years ago. I still teach one course per week and go to school on the weekends. The course I teach is preparing me for a more sophisticated teaching position once I graduate.

A crucial requirement for all doctoral programs is the notorious doctoral dissertation. The doctoral dissertation is similar to the master's thesis but is more comprehensive, detailed, strenuous, and meaningful. Students take on this project that can take anywhere from two to five years to complete because the data gathering process can be difficult depending on the study methodology. A student by the name of Lori explained,

> I had to travel to China to gather data on my participants. Each day, I would have detailed conversations with the people of China which became difficult because of the language barrier. I had to hire a translator, and I would record all of my conversations. I spent three summers in China for my fieldwork which became a financial burden.

The doctoral dissertation topic should be chosen ahead of time and should be chosen strategically. Some conduct a quantitative research study while others conduct a qualitative research study. Many believe that qualitative research studies yield more credible information. One professor of anthropology explained the following,

> If I were conducting a study on people who touched their face and simply handed out a survey, my study would only give me a numerical count [mean, median, standard deviation] which does not have much substance. If I had a conversation with each person, I would learn why each

person touched their face. In this case, a qualitative research study would be more powerful and meaningful.

Regardless of a student's research methodology, a doctoral dissertation is highly research oriented and will help others understand more about a specific topic. The following Pert Network example used in project management illustrates the different stages of the doctoral dissertation and the master's thesis project along with the estimated amount of time to complete each project. It should be mentioned that this process may look different, depending on the institution, degree, and program.

Figure 5 - Stages of Thesis/Dissertation Process
(Pert Network Example)

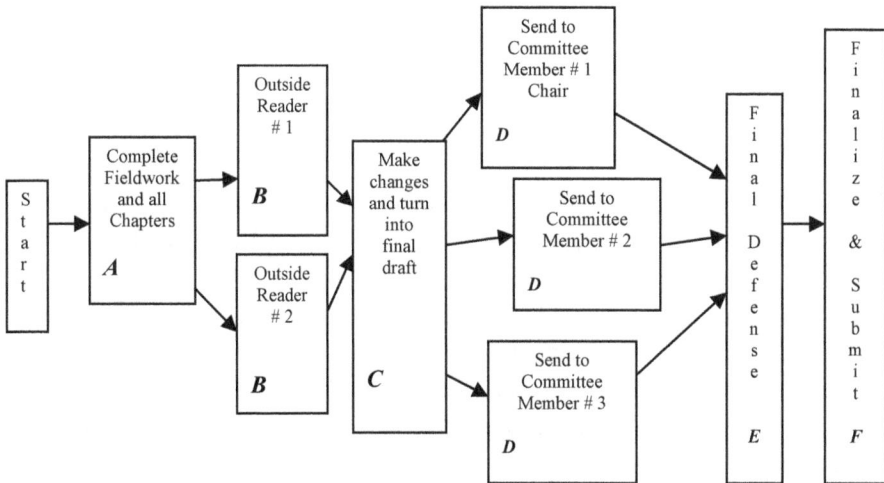

Table 4 - Approximate Timeframe to Complete a Dissertation or Thesis Research Study

Program	Start to Stage A	Stage A to B	Stage B to C	Stage C to D	Stage D to E	Stage E to F
Dissertation	2 years	2 months	3 months	2 months	3 months	2 months
Thesis	1 year	1 month	1 month	2 months	1 month	1 month

Post-Doctoral Research Programs

Post-doctoral research programs are on the rise because of the growing competition in academia. A post-doctoral program offers specialized training in a specific subject matter, endless research opportunities to publish with scholars in the field, and experience teaching courses at the undergraduate and graduate level. For many, post-doctoral programs are unnecessary while for others, it's a priceless experience. A post-doctoral student by the name of David explained the following,

> I earned my doctoral degree at a very young age because of my planning skills. As a result, I decided to start a post-doc program where I could sharpen my skills in conducting research and teaching. I figured this would be a smart decision considering there are so many baby boomers in the academic world who will be retiring within the next couple of years.

With baby boomers (born in between 1946-1964) getting ready to retire from the workforce, the generation Y (born after 1980, also known as the "Millennial Generation") are ready to take over those positions. Those who have completed post-doctoral programs will be more competitive and will have an upper hand when applying for positions. Each year, a limited number of students are admitted into post-doctoral programs. A student by the name of Jessica explained her post-doctoral program,

> It was a demanding program that developed me into an expert in my field. A post-doctoral program is similar to a medical doctor's residency where a doctor receives specialized training in a specific field. I was also able to do a lot of networking as a post-doc student.

A post-doctoral program appointment can be anywhere from one to three years long. One job positing stated,

> The Graduate School of Business anticipates appointing one Postdoctoral Fellow for a period of two years. The

Postdoctoral Fellow will collaborate in research projects of mutual interest with the faculty. In addition, the Postdoctoral Fellow will teach two sections per year of MBA level courses.

Each school and department will have specific expectations of what a post-doctoral researcher will be required to do. Some programs provide a stipend, while others provide intrinsic rewards. For example, a university advertised the following,

Fellows must have earned their doctoral degree no earlier than January 2004 and no later than June 2010. The Fellowship provides a stipend of $53,000, standard fringe benefits, a one-time moving allowance of $1,500, plus a research budget of $2,000. All Fellows will be housed in relevant home departments for which they teach two courses per year (one in winter and one in the spring quarter).

With education being so important, many spend countless years learning and mastering their fields. A person who is committed to success will sacrifice many years to education in return for a more promising future. Earning an undergraduate degree takes about four years, a master's degree takes about two years, a doctoral level degree takes about four years, and a post-doctoral degree can take another two years. With global competition, the elite student can anticipate going to school for 12 years and earning multiple graduate level degrees.

Summary

This chapter focused on graduate education. Many agree that endurance is a key factor in being successful in graduate school. Graduate school turns students into efficient multi-taskers who are capable of taking on many different projects.

Chapter Four Discussion Questions

1. What are the benefits of having a graduate level degree?
2. Why is it so important to pay close attention to a university's accreditation?
3. What can a pert network chart be used for?
4. How are jobs of the future different from jobs of today? What sorts of skills and knowledge will be required of workers?
5. How can a student start preparing for a graduate level exam ahead of time?

CHAPTER 5

Online Education

"It has become appallingly obvious that our technology has exceeded our humanity." — Albert Einstein

*O*nline education is becoming more prevalent throughout the world as students have the luxury of completing programs without physically being in a classroom. As a matter of fact, online education has been around for nearly three decades, and Nova Southeastern University (NSU) was the first higher education institution to offer graduate programs in an online format (Mujtaba, 2007, p.46). Interestingly enough, Nova Southeastern University has been offering online programs since 1983. Online education has allowed millions of students to complete their education in a non-traditional format that has resulted in many debates. Some believe that online education is unfair and unjust because students do not learn the course objectives. Others have mentioned how online educators are disconnected from their students. The reality is that online education has proven to be successful, convenient, and beneficial based upon years of research by educators and administrators which is precisely why online education is becoming more prevalent. It must be mentioned that many universities also offer hybrid programs where students are required to come to class and participate in an online platform as specified by the instructor. Several examples of online platforms that have been used in education are Blackboard, Web CT, and Ning. Each platform is unique and enables an instructor or facilitator to plan, organize, lead, and control the learning outcomes and objectives of the course. In 2009, California State University, East Bay implemented an AACSB accredited online undergraduate program in Business Administration. The university website states, "The only AACSB-accredited Online Business Administration degree completion program offered by a California university that offers adults the knowledge and skills necessary to understand the changing global business environment and prepare them for success in their professional careers." As such, being an online student requires dedication, motivation, and the ability to complete tasks with limited guidance and direction.

Online Students

Deciding to be an online student is a serious commitment. Those who have discipline are able to handle the demands of an online course while reaping the many benefits. For example, most organizations depend upon computer savvy individuals who are able to utilize specific software programs for completing tasks in an efficient manner. Furthermore, organizations depend on individuals who can constantly adapt to new technologies to help reduce errors. Thus, it makes logical sense for students to be highly knowledgeable with computers and capable of producing high quality work without much guidance. A college instructor explained,

> I have two graduate level degrees. I received my first graduate degree from a traditional university and my second graduate degree from a non-traditional university where I completed my program online. I can honestly tell you that I worked twice as hard for my second graduate level degree that was completed online. In both programs, I graduated with honors. Being an online student is strenuous but rewarding. As a result, I prefer hybrid programs.

Hybrid programs can be extremely beneficial for most courses and programs. For example, many local colleges offer a hybrid speech course where students complete the majority of their coursework online and are required to come in once a week to deliver a speech to their peers. Many other colleges who offer hybrid courses require their students to come in on exam days. An online student by the name of Robert stated,

Being an online student has allowed me to keep my job while going to school. I do not have the comfort of going to a traditional university where I sit in the classroom and learn. I take my classes online and have trained myself to learn new theories based upon the information that is provided to me. Of course, when I have questions, I can easily send my instructors an email.

Many believe that online education can be extremely beneficial for adult learners (*andragogy*) as oppose to child learners (*pedagogy*) because adult learners can draw upon their knowledge and experiences from different fields. Adult learners are encouraged to make connections and use their prior knowledge to grasp new concepts. Over the years, many students have completed their undergraduate, graduate, and even doctoral degrees online and have spent over $120,000 on tuition fees. This phenomenon is becoming more prevalent and may become the status quo of the future. Online education can be expensive and unfortunately, some programs overcharge their students. There are currently many "*diploma mills*" where students can purchase a degree online. Students should pay close attention to the institution's accreditation when deciding on specific programs. It must be mentioned that colleges and universities who offer programs online are able to accommodate at least 30-40 students per course. Hypothetically, if each student pays $2,000 per course, the institution is making well over $70,000 per course and of that $70,000, a faculty member who is required to do all of the work can expect to make less than 5% of that large sum. If a college or university offers 100 courses online per year, and is able to profit at least $50,000 per course, the total profit is $5,000,000, yes, five million dollars annually. That explains why there are so many diploma mills.

Online Faculty

Online faculty members are usually instructors who are looking for additional experience, extra income, or may be full time faculty who specialize in online education. They are responsible for teaching or facilitating a course or two every term. Generally speaking, instructors spend about 15-25 hours per week teaching online courses. Depending on the college or university, online faculty members usually have limited interactions with their students. One adjunct online instructor stated,

> I have been teaching online for about five years now and for the most part, I enjoy it. I am usually overwhelmed with emails from students who have questions. Also, it takes a lot of time to grade papers. I really feel disconnected from my students and miss being in the traditional classroom. Everything is so standardized, and I have no say on how things should be done.

Online instructors are usually required to take an orientation course prior to teaching an online course. The orientation course introduces the instructor to the different mediums of communication, how to check for plagiarism, how to grade papers using rubrics, and ultimately, how to facilitate the course efficiently and effectively. Many retired professors have come back to academia to teach online. Some professors teach at a number of colleges or universities and make well over $100,000 a year. Imagine making $100,000 a year and not having to ever leave the house. Some believe that online faculty members have it pretty easy while others believe that online faculty members deserve more recognition, income, and academic freedom. An online instructor explained the following,

> Teaching online is a lot of fun. I am continuously learning. I have students from all over the world. The majority of my students live in a different time zone, which I find very interesting. I am always looking for additional courses to teach.

The student evaluations at the end of each term are what measure the success of online instructors. This means that if an instructor is teaching a number of courses for different colleges and universities, he or she cannot neglect any student in any way because at the end of each term, students are usually required to take an online survey where they evaluate the quality of education, the attentiveness of the instructor, and whether or not they would recommend the instructor. An online instructor must be extremely efficient because all assignments must be graded by a certain date and time, all emails must be responded to within 24-48 hours, and all issues must be dealt with in a timely manner. Successful online instructors will have the required educational background to teach a course, practical experience in the field he or she is teaching, research publications in the field he or she is teaching, and will have above average computer and technological skills.

Technology

Many online programs have invested in resources to help create a more interconnected virtual classroom. For example, several universities have implemented VoIP (Voice over Internet Protocol) in each course so instructors can lecture "live" and students can ask questions. Of course, this requires both the instructor and the students to be on the course website simultaneously. Other colleges and universities have used *YouTube* as a medium for communicating and explaining concepts. A new and growing wave of instructional resources is offered online for those who want to see the practical implications of a concept or theory used in a society. For instance, if an economics instructor is teaching the concept of supply and demand to his or her students who are visual and kinesthetic learners, the instructor can easily click on an internet link where a real life example of supply and demand is demonstrated by showing how demand increases or decreases based upon the price of tickets at a baseball game. These educational tools have helped instructors teach difficult concepts to a diverse group of learners with different learning styles. With technology constantly evolving, online education has proven to be effective and convenient for both students and instructors.

Virtual Education

With online education becoming more prevalent, many question whether or not degrees that are earned from online colleges and universities are weighted equally to degrees earned from traditional universities. A professor of sociology stated the following,

> If one has earned all of one's degrees online, then that individual will most likely be qualified to teach in online programs as oppose to traditional on-ground programs. At

this time, I would recommend a student to obtain all of his or her degrees the traditional way and to have an additional online degree. This way the individual will have all of the bases covered and will be more employable.

Being able to advance in the corporate world with an online degree is highly possible. For example, there are many first-line managers who have undergraduate degrees and want to be promoted to middle-management positions without having to physically go to a classroom several times a week. Many end up enrolling in a graduate online program. A marketing director explained,

> I was very fortunate to be able to complete my MBA program online because it contributed to my promotion at work. There was no way I could have completed my program the traditional way because of my different obligations. My next goal is to earn a doctoral degree online and strategically position myself for a VP position.

Earning a degree online will definitely help those who are working in the corporate world but can limit those who are interested in working in academia.

Summary

This chapter provided information on online education. Online education is definitely becoming more prevalent throughout the world. As a result, more students are able to complete their educational objectives.

Chapter Five Discussion Questions

1. What have you heard about online education?
2. How would you feel if you found out that your teacher or professor received his or her degrees from an online institution?
3. What sorts of skills are required in an online setting that would be different from a traditional classroom?
4. What are the pros and cons to an online education?

5. Look through your favorite college's schedule of classes. What online courses are offered that would be of interest to you?

CHAPTER 6

Vocational Education

"Everything should be made as simple as possible, but not simpler."
—Albert Einstein

Vocational education is becoming more prevalent for students throughout the world. Students who prefer to learn and master a vocation go to a vocational or career oriented school where they are trained to start a career upon graduation. The difference between a vocational school and a traditional university or college is that a vocational school is career oriented and teaches a student a specific skill. Some believe there is a stigma behind going to a vocational school but in reality, vocational schools produce high-quality and skilled workers who contribute significantly to the workforce. Many vocational schools offer fast-paced programs that last anywhere from six months to two years. Many vocational schools require students to complete an internship or externship before graduating which helps students put the theory they have learned into practice. Also, the experience gained through an externship or internship helps students acquire the confidence that is needed to be successful in their new careers. The reality is that many students go to a four-year traditional college and then are unable to find work in their field because they were never given the opportunity from a practical perspective to put the information they have learned to use. At a vocational school, many of the students who complete their internship or externship are usually hired by the site where they interned because they have already built rapport and have proven to be extraordinary workers. Most vocational schools and programs are accredited and go through extensive programmatic reviews by their accrediting bodies on a regular basis.

Vocational education may not be for everyone; however, it has the potential to be a great option for those who need a quicker path to start a career.

Vocational Education Programs

Vocational schools offer many different programs to accommodate students with different interests. Most vocational programs require students to have a high school diploma. In recent years, many programs have become "impacted" (meaning they have more students wanting to declare that major than can be accommodated), which has forced students to be waitlisted. Many see the benefits of going to a vocational college and learning a specific skill, obtaining hands-on training, and in some cases, earning a degree.

There are a myriad of vocational programs available to students. For example, students have the choice of studying pharmacy technology, construction, medical assisting, dental assisting, nursing, massage therapy, graphic design, radiology technology, respiratory therapy, sonography, computers, criminal justice, veterinary technology, and many other interesting fields. Many vocational schools also offer career placement upon graduation. A medical assistant named Maria stated the following,

> I am happy that I decided to go to a vocational college after high school because I was able to learn a new set of skills and enter the workforce immediately. Some of my friends who went to a traditional college have changed their majors several times and have not made any progress with their education. I currently work at a hospital and enjoy going to work each day.

With the job market becoming more specialized, government agencies and businesses are investing more in the future of vocational programs to help balance the supply and demand. Many vocational schools are focusing on providing high-end programs needed in the health field, such as: nuclear medicine, radiation therapy, and electro neuro-diagnostic technology. Students who graduate from such high-end programs are in high-demand and do not have to worry about acquiring multiple graduate level degrees, publishing in peer-reviewed journals, or spending more than a decade in school. Teresa, who is a nuclear medicine technologist, explained the following,

> I was able to become a certified nuclear medicine technologist within two years of completing the prerequisites. This field is consistently growing, and I am fortunate to have such a great job that pays so well. I do not have any regrets and have both job security and stability for the rest of my working career. I actually make more than my friends who have graduate level degrees.

Students are starting to realize that traditional colleges and universities are unable to provide job placement for their students and as a result, many students are left with a college degree, school loans, and unemployment. This phenomenon has become more apparent during the current economic crisis which has not impacted professionals in the health field. A radiology technologist named Joey stated, "I am currently working a lot of overtime at the hospital. I think more people are becoming sick and depressed due to the current state of the economy, which is providing me with more work. It is bittersweet." At the end of the day, it is important for a student to do his or her research ahead of time by figuring out what fields are in high-demand.

Curriculum

The curriculum at vocational colleges and schools are robust and vigorous. Students are expected to learn and retain a significant amount of information in a small period of time. At a traditional college or university, students are either on a semester or quarter system. A semester system is approximately eighteen weeks long and a quarter system is approximately ten weeks long. Most vocational colleges and schools use a modular term system that runs approximately six weeks. It is important to mention that it is not the length of the semester, quarter, or term that is important but rather the hours that are spent in a classroom. For example, if a student is going to a traditional college or university that is on a semester system (18 weeks) and is taking two courses and is expected to be in each course once a week for three hours, the student will receive a total of 108 hours of class time instruction for two courses. If a different student is enrolled at a vocational college that is on the modular term system (6 weeks) and is expected to be in class four times a week for a total of four and a half hours each day, the student will receive 108 hours of class time instruction per term. Thus, those who are on the modular term system are on the fast-track and cannot fall behind. A student named Jessica stated the following,

> I enjoy the fast-paced system at my vocational college. I don't have time to mess up, and it keeps me on my toes. I need structure and a routine to follow; otherwise, I will go astray. I am also noticing that I am learning more because I am being challenged each day.

The truth is that students need to be constantly challenged in order to learn and retain information. If a class only meets once a week, there are six days in between each class where the student can easily forget valuable information because with memory, if a person does not use it, he or she can lose it. Vocational programs are investing in their curriculum by following the strict rules and regulations of their elite accrediting bodies. For example, vocational programs have enhanced their learning objectives for each course, implemented learning outcomes for each course, and have standardized the entire curriculum for each program.

Many do not fully understand the difference between course objectives and outcomes. A simple definition for course objectives can be the course goals that are usually listed on the course syllabus. A simple definition for a course learning outcome is what a student will be able to do at the completion of the course. Learning outcomes are the current popular trend in education because they allow an educational environment to continuously improve in all aspects of learning and teaching. Many vocational colleges have implemented pre-tests and post-tests that measure how much a student has learned after taking a class with a specific instructor. This not only puts pressure on the instructor but also on the student. Instructors no longer have as much academic freedom because they are now focused on the assessment that each student takes at the end of a class to determine what was learned. On the other hand, students must do well because a significant percentage of their grade is on the line with the end of term assessment. By default, instructors and students must put more effort into the class. Critics of learning outcomes have pointed out that learning outcomes are neither fair nor accurate because certain matters (student retention and student motivation) are not taken into consideration. A director of a vocational college named Roger shared the following story,

> We had a math instructor who got along very well with students and staff. At the end of each course, the majority of his students would receive A's and he would never have anyone who failed. He was also known for always letting his class out early but because the majority of his students received high marks in his class, we were under the impression that he was an outstanding instructor. We implemented a math learning outcome (pre-test and post-test) in his class to measure how much students were actually learning. On the first week of class, the pre-test was given out and a total of 5% of his students were able to pass the exam. On the last week of class, the post-test was given out, and only 20% of the class was able to pass the exam. We were greatly disappointed with the learning outcome results. Our other math instructor who taught a different section of the same course also used the pre-test and post-test method, and on the first day of class, only 5% of his students passed the pre-test, and on the last day of class, 90% of his students were able to pass the post-test.

Instructors take on a big responsibility when they are in the classroom because they are constantly being evaluated and must be able to please all constituencies. Not only do students and supervisors rate instructors but now learning outcomes rate how well an instructor is performing as well.

Instructors

Instructors at vocational schools and colleges are highly trained professionals who have a passion for their profession. The majority of the instructors have a significant amount of work experience (10 or more years) but do not necessarily have high levels of education. For example, a criminal justice instructor could have 20 years of experience as a police officer but may only have an associate's degree. To teach at a vocational college or school, experience is important because it is the responsibility of the instructor to be able to teach a student a specific skill. To be a successful vocational instructor, an individual needs to have sound technical, human, and conceptual skills that assist an instructor with teaching complex information in a short period of time. Many vocational colleges and schools have implemented educational incentive programs where instructors are reimbursed for continuing with their education. As a result, each year more and more instructors are enrolling into graduate level programs. A vocational instructor by the name of Jasmine explained the following,

> I have over 15 years of experience as a medical assistant. For the longest time, I didn't want to continue with my education and felt that my associate's degree was enough. After some research, I learned that I could receive a bachelor's degree in the field of Education to help me as an instructor. I am currently taking courses that are fine-tuning my teaching capabilities and providing me with more confidence in the classroom.

Vocational colleges are also encouraging their instructors to obtain higher levels of education because accrediting bodies are requesting that instructors have both the experience (professionally qualified) and the education (academically qualified).

Summary

Vocational education is flourishing and the benefits are becoming more noticeable to the general public. Many students do not have the time to spend four to ten years in a traditional school without a guaranteed position waiting for them upon graduation. Students who have graduated from vocational colleges and schools learn a specific skill in a short period of time that will help them start a career.

Chapter Six Discussion Questions

1. Why is vocational education becoming more popular both nationally and internationally?
2. What are the drawbacks to a vocational education?
3. Should vocational education curriculum be standardized?

CHAPTER 7

Mentoring and Networking

"Only a life lived for others is a life worthwhile."
—Albert Einstein

*M*entoring and networking are two important aspects of educational success. Throughout school, a student should have a mentor who is able to give him or her advice. Also, students are expected to network with their peers throughout school. Both mentoring and networking play a big role in the outcome of one's educational journey. Those who do not have a mentor end up wasting a significant amount of time trying to figure things out on their own. On the same note, those who do not network are unable to take advantage of the many benefits of being well connected to others. The best example of this is seen in many organizations where potential applicants are referred to hiring managers by current employees. In his classic 1974 study *Getting a Job*, sociologist Mark Granovetter looked at several hundred professional and technical workers from the Boston suburb of Newton, interviewing them in some detail on their employment history. He found that "56 percent of those he talked to found their job through a personal connection" (Gladwell, 2002, p. 54). Developing personal connections is a skill that cannot be overlooked because in the real world, knowing the right people can open up many doors and opportunities. Mentoring is a cycle that continues. Those who have been mentored eventually become mentors because they can recall their own experiences of needing practical advice and understand the importance of having a mentor. Being a mentor allows an individual to form a strong bond with his or her mentee, which is built upon respect, trust, and knowledge.

Mentoring

Finding the right mentor can be a difficult task. It is important to find a mentor who an individual can relate to and who can relate to the individual. A mentor is someone who a person can go to when he or she needs guidance because the mentor is usually older, wiser, and has experienced similar situations. This does not mean that the mentor is always right and the mentee does not have a right to challenge the mentor. There needs to be a mutual understanding that the mentor and mentee will discuss topics and make informed decisions collectively. A successful graduate student named Linda explained the importance of having a mentor,

> My mentor and I meet on a regular basis. My mentor received his doctoral degree from the same university and program in which I am currently enrolled. He has shared valuable tips on what to do and what to be aware of. If it was not for him, I wouldn't have made it this far. I am also able to talk to him about non-academic affairs. I would strongly urge all students to have a mentor with whom they can speak openly.

In low-context cultures, parents usually play the role of a mentor and are able to assist their children with any questions they may have. In high-context cultures, children cannot discuss certain matters that can be "embarrassing" with their parents and are forced to seek advice elsewhere. For example, a young adult from a high-context culture like Japan or Saudi Arabia usually cannot discuss personal feelings with his or her parent(s). A college student named Mary explained,

> My parents are unable to help me when I have questions or need advice about my education because they are unfamiliar with the educational system here in America. My favorite teacher in high school has become my mentor and has helped me in specific areas that my parents are unable to assist. My teacher and I have developed a strong bond, and I am grateful for his advice.

Many immigrants face situations where they need mentors who understand the demands and expectations of a society. At times, immigrant students from high-context cultures have no choice but to appoint their father as their mentor (out of respect) in all areas of life, which can become a risky dynamic. A graduate student by the name of Sal explained,

> I had no choice but to elect my father as my mentor, and as a result, I am living a miserable life that fulfilled all of my father's dreams and none of my own. He chose my occupation, wife, and lifestyle for me. My culture emphasizes the importance of respecting parents, and I am basically stuck.

The point here is that a mentor does not necessarily have to be a family member. At times, it can be a better choice to have a mentor who is from a different culture with different beliefs who can give an individual a different perspective on life.

The mentoring system is also used in organizations for individuals who are new to the organization or are interested in becoming managers. An individual is teamed up with a senior employee or current manager and is exposed to the tasks that are required to be successful in a specific position. This strategy has helped many employees quickly adapt to positions. Mentors need the following characteristics: strong interpersonal skills, accumulated knowledge, strong servant leadership skills, sense of personal power, ability to maintain confidentiality, and a willingness to be patient and supportive.

Networking

Networking is a skill that is taught in most graduate programs because of its relevance to success. Psychologist Stanley Milgram conducted a research study on how well people are connected where he proposed the concept of six degrees of separation. "Six degrees of separation doesn't mean that everyone is linked to everyone in just six steps. It means that a very small number of people are linked to everyone else in a few steps, and the rest of us are linked to the world through those specific few" (Gladwell, 2002, p. 37). Being able to network gives people access to opportunities and worlds to which they do not belong. Those who have implemented networking into their everyday lives are consistently building relationships and connecting with different groups or sub-groups. Being connected means that a person will have endless contacts that can potentially assist an individual in different ways. By having a diverse group of peers, colleagues, friends, and acquaintances, a person will be exposed to different ideas, perspectives, and information. When looking for a job or a second job, a person can easily send out a massive email to all of the people he or she knows to see if they are able to assist. At many organizations, managers expect employees to refer strong external candidates to their departments because if an employee is a good worker, then the chances are that the person they are recommending will also have the same work ethic. Just by socializing, someone can be easily networking. Even the people who do not feel comfortable networking or socializing with strangers should consider the importance of being well connected in this competitive global society. As a matter of fact, social networking websites have become more prevalent and are used strategically by many professionals.

Social networking sites such as Linkedin.com or Facebook.com have millions of users who are trying to network with others by using the internet as a medium of connecting with people all over the world. Social networking sites are also a way for a person to market his or her abilities. Many entrepreneurs have opened up accounts on social networking sites and have promoted their products, skills, and services. For example, a car dealer named Daniel explained the following:

> I opened up a Facebook account so I could promote my services. As a result, I have been able to reach out to more potential customers, and my lucrative business is flourishing. I don't have to pay a dime, and I can advertise for free.

Although social networking sites are helpful, many still believe that "word of mouth" is the most powerful medium for networking. Networking has three branches that are all equally as important. The first branch is knowing a lot of people (social), the second branch is knowing a lot of people with authority (political), and the third is knowing a lot of people that can help you financially (economical).

Knowing a lot of people means being connected in a human web. Knowing a lot of people can help students when they are conducting research studies and need participants or when they are organizing a conference and need volunteers. From a social perspective, knowing a lot of people can have an impact on a person's social life. Many have benefited from this social phenomenon and have met their "significant other" through friends of friends. A doctoral student named Tim stated,

> My college roommate introduced me to his group of friends, and I started to hang out with them while I was in college. After college, the same group of friends introduced me to a girl to whom I am now happily married. I would have never met my wife if my college roommate hadn't introduced me to his group of friends.

Just by knowing a lot of people, a person will automatically increase his or her chances in many situations and, by default, end up meeting people with authority.

Knowing people with authority is important in this society because those with authority can make big changes. Managers are a prime example of having authority because managers have authority to hire. The more managers a person knows, the more likely that he or she will be able to find employment opportunities. A civil engineer named Richard stated the following,

> After I graduated with my undergraduate degree in civil engineering, I thought I wouldn't have any troubles finding work, and I was completely wrong. Unfortunately, I did not have significant work experience in my field and that was an issue. I let my mentor know about the situation, and he was able to make some phone calls for me. Within a week, I was offered a position as a junior civil engineer at the same firm from which my mentor retired.

From a political perspective, finding and meeting people with authority can be difficult but is definitely possible. It's a matter of networking and having the right allies.

Knowing a lot of people can help a person financially when he or she is looking for a good deal on a product or service. Many people ask around before they buy a new product by trying to find the best deal. At times, people are able to find a friend of a friend who works at a store and are able to use their employee discount to purchase the product. A graduate student by the name of Tiffany stated the following,

> I needed a new laptop and decided to ask around to see if any of my friends could help me find a decent laptop for a fair price. A friend mentioned that his brother was working at some electronics store, so we went there to check out some of the laptops. I was able to find a laptop that I liked and was able to purchase it with a 20% discount by using his discount. I saved a total of $200 just by asking around.

Networking has been proven to help individuals from a social, political, and economical perspective. Mastering the art of networking can only open up more opportunities for success.

Summary

This chapter focused on the importance of mentoring and networking. Those who take advantage of mentoring and networking will have more opportunities in life. Those who have more opportunities in life will most likely be more successful and will be able to give back to others.

Chapter Seven Discussion Questions

1. Who is your mentor and why did you choose this person to be your mentor?
2. Why is it important to have a mentor in life? Can someone have more than one mentor?
3. What characteristics do you think a mentor should have?

4. What are some strategies you can use to network? Name one upcoming or existing opportunity to network for yourself.
5. Who are some people you know who are well connected? Do they have a certain type of personality?

CHAPTER 8

Conversations with Professionals

"Learn from yesterday, live for today, hope for tomorrow. The
important thing is not to stop questioning."
—Albert Einstein

*T*hose who are aware and prepared for situations usually
outperform their competitors. For example, those who play sports
understand that continuous practice will help athletes perform better
because they will have the endurance, stamina, and physical and mental
capabilities to perform at higher levels. The same is true when going in
for an interview or when taking an exam. Those who are prepared will
almost always surpass those who are not. Being prepared for an
educational journey cannot be stressed enough, and as a matter of fact,
is not stressed enough. Many believe that the educational journey is
relaxed and that everyone is a winner. This false notion has left many
individuals in despair because the educational journey is intense,
competitive, and full of obstacles. It is very important to have
successful mentors throughout an educational journey who can give a
person effective advice on what to do and what not to do. Those who
are the first in their family to earn a college degree or to go to graduate
school endure an enormous amount of stress and frustration because
they do not have someone in their immediate family who can guide
them through this unique phase. Ellen Herda, an anthropologist and
professor at the University of San Francisco explained, "For every
conversation there is a common language or there is the creation of a
common language among interlocutors" (1999, p. 121). The following
conversations with selected professionals provide useful information

that will give the reader some examples of successful journeys toward educational goals.

The Medical Doctor

Sultana Laila Sultani received her BA at the University of California, Berkeley, where she majored in Middle Eastern Studies while concurrently fulfilling her pre-medical requisites. She graduated from The George Washington University School of Medicine in 2009 and is a resident physician specializing in Ob/GYN at Santa Clara Valley Medical Center in San Jose.

BK: What made you decide to become a medical doctor, and what characteristics are needed to become a successful medical doctor?

SS: My grandmother was a strong woman. "I'm from the mountains," she would say when questioned about her ability to remain steadfast through war in Afghanistan, refugee status in India, and poverty in America. However, I witnessed her strength falter for the first time when news arrived from Kabul announcing the death of her niece during childbirth, leaving a husband widowed and young children motherless. My grandmother quickly regained her composure, but those fleeting moments of weakness were unsettling. I would soon learn that these tragedies were not uncommon for Afghans and that, in fact, Afghanistan endured one of the highest maternal mortality rates in the world. Although I was born and raised in America, my grandmother had instilled in me the desire to help the women of Afghanistan. It was as early as the fifth grade, when I was assigned to write a career report, that I learned the vehicle by which I would reach this dream.

"What are you good at?" It was a simple question intended to lead students to the most compatible career. Never the athlete, theatrical star, or musician, I was instead deemed by my family, friends, and teachers as a "nurturer". I was the unyielding teacher's aid, my parents' helping hand, and the unconditionally devoted sister. It was this innate tendency to care for the well-being of others that led me to explore the health profession.

During my career report presentation at eleven years of age, I announced that I would become a doctor dedicated to women's health when I grew up. I was the only kid in my class who knew what Ob/GYN [Obstetrics-Gynecology] even stood for. Over a decade of schooling later, I have maintained my focus and have grown even more determined to meet these very same career aspirations.

My grandmother passed away during my second year in medical school, but she is always with me. I credit her and her stories of a country torn, of a people broken, and of the needless death of so many women for stirring something in me that grew into the will and motivation I possess today.

BK: How did you decide on your specialty?

SS: The first experience of night float on L&D (Labor and Delivery) clinched my decision to pursue a career in Ob/GYN. This specialty had everything I sought from a profession—medical challenges, invigorating procedures, continuity of care, women's health, and the privilege to delve into the very private world of women, witnessing the miracle of birth, and catching a glimpse of the sacred bond between mother and child.

BK: What do you plan on doing with your specialized training?

SS: Ultimately, I hope to use the knowledge and skill to not only improve the state of women's health in my community here in America but also to provide for the people from the land of my ancestors. Though years have passed since I originally heard stories of the plight of Afghan women, the dire need for health care reform in Afghanistan has not abated. I am under no illusions that my contribution will cure all ailments or correct all deficits of the health care system. Rather, I choose to be practical and pragmatic. I believe that by providing education and training to doctors, nurses, and midwives, I can reach many more than I would alone. I am confident that simple training coupled with only minor changes in protocol and access to affordable supplies can help women's healthcare in Afghanistan rise above the limitations of its current condition.

BK: How can a student start preparing for medical school in high school?

SS: Learn your study skills early. It is important to be disciplined and structured on a daily basis. After class, immediately do your homework and review new topics of the day. This is the only way to reinforce your learning. Also, try to be involved in extra-curricular activities, such as: tutoring, sports, and volunteering. These are all important in contributing to self-growth.

BK: How many years after high school are required to become a medical doctor?

SS: On average, it takes eight years after high school to become a medical doctor. This includes approximately four years of college and four years of medical school. Some choose to take the non-traditional route by extending their college education with double majors, completing a Master's degree in a health related field, and getting job experience prior to applying to medical school, which can lengthen the time for completion.

BK: How important is it for someone to major in a field related to science in college?

SS: This is merely a matter of preference. There are a set of required classes one must complete in college, which can be credited toward a science major. However, you can opt to do the requirements and have a non-science major. For instance, I majored in Middle Eastern Studies at UC Berkeley.

BK: How important is one's GPA in college?

SS: It is very important. Getting accepted into medical school is very challenging and competitive. Your GPA is a reflection of your overall study skills and knowledge base.

BK: As an undergraduate, what were some of your difficult classes and how did you pass them?

SS: General Chemistry and Physics were especially challenging for me. I spent many hours at the library, while most of my friends enjoyed the social scene. I would spend quality time in the student learning center, which offered student tutoring that was especially helpful in breaking down large new topics. The key is discipline, and staying organized and committed to a well-planned schedule.

BK: What exams did you have to take to get into medical school and how did you prepare for them?

SS: In addition to all the mid-terms and finals for each class in college, you also have to take the MCAT. This is a standardized exam that encompasses all the topics covered during pre-medical required courses. There are several exam prep classes offered that most people utilize. For example, there is Kaplan and Princeton Review. I used one of these courses to direct my studies.

BK: Describe the medical school interview process.

SS: Medical school interviews vary depending on the institution you are visiting. Students have interviews with faculty, deans, as well as with medical students. The interview group is typically taken on a tour of the facilities and hospital and given time for Q&A with medical school representatives.

BK: Tell me about your experiences with medical school.

SS: I thoroughly enjoyed my medical school experience. The first two years are classroom based and are very much like learning a new language. Because the classes are relatively small, you create strong bonds with your peers. The last two years are spent in the wards of the hospital. This time offers you a glimpse of every specialty and allows you to finally put into action all the knowledge cultivated during the first two years in medical school.

BK: Tell me about your experiences with your residency and how that determines your specialty.

SS: In the fourth year of medical school, students select their specialty of choice. It is at that time that medical students apply to residency programs across the nation. Residency, ranging from three to seven years depending on the chosen specialty, offers intense training to the physician.

BK: What advice/tips would you give a student who is interested in becoming a medical doctor?

SS: Sometimes the long road to attaining your MD can be daunting. Focus on the task at hand while keeping your ultimate goal in mind to motivate you. Do well in high school, so that you can get into a good college. Do well in college, so that you can get into a good medical school. Do well in medical school, so that you can be a good doctor. Be a good doctor, so that you can do well for your patients.

BK: What does a typical day at work look like for you?

SS: In Labor and Delivery, the day starts before sunrise. We see our entire list of patients who have stayed overnight in the hospital. They are those who recently delivered, had an operation, or are ill for other reasons. Once those patients are evaluated, and their medical plan for the day is set, we move on to care for our laboring patients. After a set of teaching rounds, the remainder of the day is spent doing vaginal deliveries and surgeries including cesarean sections. This is my experience as a resident physician in Ob/GYN. Other specialties have their own distinct set of residency experiences.

The Civil Engineer

Nelofar Horakhsh was born in Kabul, Afghanistan, and moved with her family to the Bay Area of California when she was six months old. She earned her B.S. in Civil Engineering with a Minor in Mathematics from San Jose State University and is working toward her P.E. license for the State of California. She currently works for a private consulting firm in Silicon Valley that does design work for various transportation and development projects throughout the state.

Her professional interests include green building, sustainability, and transportation solutions.

BK: What made you decide to become an engineer?

NH: Initially, I had entered college for a major in computer engineering, but after 9/11 and the ongoing war in Afghanistan, I saw the ousting of the Taliban as a potential opportunity for a democratic Afghanistan. I figured a time would come where there would be more stability in Afghanistan, and I could go back and help re-build. I felt I would be better able to contribute to the re-building efforts in Afghanistan as a civil engineer, and so I changed my major halfway through my college career to civil engineering.

BK: What characteristics are needed to become a successful engineer?

NH: I believe that the willingness to learn and having a good work ethic are essential to being successful in any career path, including civil engineering. However, realistically, I think it is important to have a strong math and science foundation to make it through the required courses for the major. I realized that a lot of what I learned in college was learning how to use the resources around me to learn. You do not always have to have the answer, but you should know how to find it.

BK: How can a student start preparing for engineering in high school?

NH: It would be beneficial to take as many math and science courses as possible. Sometimes as a junior or senior, you are given the option to take additional science classes. Take advantage of your electives and do not take the easy way out by avoiding math and science.

BK: How many years after high school are required to become an engineer?

NH: It varies, depending on class availability and what university you go to, however it is generally a four to five year program. It is very difficult to finish in less than four years because of the pre-requisite requirements for many classes.

BK: How important is one's GPA in college?

NH: A good GPA does not necessarily mean an employee will be a good engineer. Often, there are people who do really well when it comes to school work (book smarts); however, they do not know how to apply their knowledge to real life (street smarts). A person's GPA is still somewhat important, though, because a bad GPA can indicate a lack of effort or ability.

BK: As an undergraduate, what were some of your difficult classes, and how did you pass them?

NH: I would have to say that my most difficult classes were the classes that had bad teachers. I am more of a classroom learner than a book learner, so I relied a lot on my professors' lectures in all of my classes. If the lecturer was a poor speaker or did not have a clear outline of what the lesson was about, I had difficulty doing well in that class. More specifically, my hardest class was a hydrology/water resources lecture. I ended up having to read the textbook as a supplemental guide to the lecture.

I would like to stress the importance of going to all lectures and labs because there is often something to be gained from the instructor like their personal experience that cannot be learned from a textbook.

BK: In retrospect, what would you have done differently in regards to coursework, exams, or experience?

NH: Almost all of my friends and colleagues say this: I could have studied more. I do not know that I would have because there is something to say about balance and the college experience. It is not all slave work and seriousness because you also need to make time to enjoy your surroundings and make friends, get involved in activities, network, and build social relationships. This will be important when you start working in the industry because you will be more confident when interacting with your peers.

BK: What advice/tips would you give a student who is interested in becoming an engineer?

NH: Knowing that there are not nearly enough students in the math and science fields, I would tell them not to be intimidated or discouraged by the amount of math, physics, and chemistry that is required for the degree. It is all do-able, so just stick to it, even if you struggle a lot. Nothing of value comes easily in life, but when you get it, it will mean so much more to you than a degree that required less effort.

BK: What is a professional engineer (PE), and why is it important?

NH: With regards to Civil Engineering, a Professional Engineer is a title that is earned after completing the following:

- Earning a four year degree from an accredited university in Civil Engineering
- Passing the eight hour national Engineer-In-Training or EIT examination
- Having a minimum of two years work experience in design (working under the supervision of a licensed Professional Engineer)
- Passing the eight hour national Professional Engineers Exam and any additional state specific exams that may be required. In California, the state specific exams include a 2.5 hour Seismic Exam for earthquake design and a 2.5 hour Surveying Exam.

Once all of these conditions have been met, you can become a licensed professional engineer. It is important to have this title if you ever want to start your own business. In order to submit plans to any government agency, you will need to have a license in order to stamp your plans. It is also important for career advancement. Most companies will not promote you above a certain level without a license.

BK: Please tell me about a typical day at work.

NH: I work for a private consulting firm that does a variety of civil work ranging from hydrology, to land development, to transportation, and surveying. My particular group works mainly in commercial land development. I spend a lot of my day doing design work using AutoCAD to design and draft utility systems and roadways. I will sometimes go to job site meetings to meet with the construction team and developers to evaluate the site and discuss project relevant information.

BK: Please explain your projects at work.

NH: Much of my work experience thus far has been in mixed-use/commercial land development. This generally consists of utility system and roadway designs for commercial buildings, shopping centers, office buildings, retail stores, restaurants, parking lots, and even residential housing and their surrounding roadways. I determine the utility layout, sizing of pipes, connections to existing systems and grading and drainage for the roadways and parking lots around buildings and structures. I have worked on large scale projects that cost hundreds of millions of dollars (an outdoor shopping center in Sunnyvale, CA), as well as small projects that only cost a few thousand dollars (add-on unit for a church in Fremont, CA). I also do contract work for Lockheed Martin Space Systems Company. I help in the design of their internal roadways and utility systems whenever there is any new construction on the Sunnyvale or Palo Alto Lockheed campuses.

The Police Officer

Adam Sayed was born and raised in the San Francisco, Bay Area of California. He has been a police officer for over four years now. In his free time, he likes to ride motorcycles, work out, and play football. When Adam is away from work, he enjoys spending time with his family friends.

BK: What made you interested in becoming a police officer?

AS: For as long as I can remember, I always wanted to be a police officer. I remember having handcuffs and toy guns as a child. My parents didn't teach me to fear the police as a young kid, and I think that's why I felt so comfortable around them. Being comfortable around police officers made me want to be one.

I was nineteen years old and in my second year at the local community college when I decided to become a police officer. I had been through about six or seven jobs by then. I thought it was time to grow up and find a career, and not just another job.

I looked to the local police department for answers to all my questions. I walked into the police department and asked the front desk personnel how I could be a police officer. The woman at the front desk smiled and asked, "Sweetie, how old are you?" I answered with pride, "Nineteen years old." She told me I was too young to be a police officer, but that I could apply for other positions within the police department. I asked for an application for an internship. Luckily, they were hiring at the time. I filled out tons of paperwork and completed several interviews. I was finally hired as an intern.

BK: What did you do as an intern?

AS: I worked the fingerprinting at the police department. I did a lot of fingerprinting for people coming in for their jobs (day cares, other police departments, schools, doctors, medical technicians, and pharmacists). I would occasionally do court ordered bookings or other criminal type fingerprinting.

The police department rotated the interns so everyone had a chance to do something new in the department. From fingerprinting to towing people's cars, I did it all as an intern. You sort of get a feel of what it is like to be a police officer and be in that environment, but at the same time it is nothing like being a police officer.

BK: How long did you work as an intern?

AS: I worked as an intern until I was twenty one years old. I finished my associate's degree at the community college I was attending and transferred to a university, about thirty minutes away. I definitely wanted to further my education while I was working at the police department. The hours at the police department were flexible, so I wasn't being overwhelmed with everything.

BK: What did you do next?

AS: I was twenty one and applied to the police department at which I was working. Most police academies require cadets to be twenty years and six months old at the start of the academy, so that when they graduate, they are twenty one years old. The police department where I was working wasn't hiring police officers at the time. I looked to a bigger agency to further my career. I filled out an interest application and waited. The part I disliked about the entire application/hiring process was all of the waiting. I guess it was because I wanted the job so much. I was so eager to start the police academy and become a police officer. I really wanted to be "one of the boys in blue."

BK: What was the process like?

AS: Most positions in police departments require several clearances before you start, especially the position of a police officer. Some of the documents I had to obtain for my application were high school transcripts, college transcripts, thorough job history records, military records (if applicable), vehicle registration, social security card, birth certificate, and medical records. Obtaining my high school and college transcripts took approximately one to two weeks. I had everything else at home already.

After I submitted all of these items, I was sent to the next step of the application process—my oral interview. I was twenty one years old and sitting in front of three supervisors and was asked several questions. All of my interviews up until then normally consisted of a casual one-on-one interview. The fact that three people were interviewing me overwhelmed me. I remember stuttering and repeatedly saying, "um" in between my answers.

The interview took about thirty minutes. They asked why I wanted the job, why I wanted to work at that particular police department, what I knew about the city and so on and so forth. They also gave me scenarios and asked me what I would do. Now there was no right or wrong answer. You just needed to have some sort of reasoning for your answers. They didn't expect me to give police officer answers. They just wanted to see what I said and what kind of reasoning I had.

I knew a lot about the city because I grew up there, so that helped out. I left the interview pretty confident. It was about four weeks before I moved onto the next step—background interview.

The background investigator asked me everything and anything about my previous jobs, my family, my neighbors, my past girlfriends, alcohol and drug history, previous arrests, and high school friends. It got annoying after a while, but I knew it was worth it in the end. I answered the questions truthfully. It is important to answer truthfully because the individual will go through a polygraph test regarding the answers from his or her background packet. Before I left the office, the background investigator asked me if he could cut some of my hair to test for narcotics (legal and illegal). He cut some hair from my head, and I was sent on my way.

I took the polygraph test about one month later and passed. Some friends ask me, "Is there a secret to passing the test?" I know the secret. It will make you pass one hundred percent. Tell the truth. You'll pass if you tell the truth. Now if you're scared of your past (drugs, alcohol, and arrests), then maybe you should hold off on applying. If you're just one of those people who get nervous about everything, just relax and answer the questions truthfully.

BK: What was the next step for you?

AS: The next step was the psychological interview. This was the most draining interview of my life. I was sent to a psychologist's office. I was directed to sit down and fill out this psychological examination. I started thumbing through the packet. There were at least twenty or thirty pages. I started filling out my answers at about 8 am and didn't finish until about 1 pm. Just sitting there made me want to go crazy. You can't really get up and walk around or do anything else. There are tons of questions that are supposed to delineate if you're mature enough or "ready" to be a police officer. They also don't want to hire anyone who will go crazy one month into being a police officer. The questions ranged from, "did you play with fire as a kid" to "do you want to kill people."

After I filled out my answers, I spoke to the psychologist. He went over my answers and asked me specific questions regarding my answers. This took about thirty minutes to an hour. He tried breaking me down during the interview. He said he thought I was "too nice" to be a police officer. I asked, "What does that mean?" That was a big mistake on my part. He took that as me being defensive and started to analyze all of my answers. At the end of the interview, he shook my hand, and said I would make a well rounded police officer. I was so confused. What had just happened? I later spoke to some people at the police department who told me he was just trying to "break me down." Thank God I didn't break down.

I was getting close to the end of the process. I had a medical examination to make sure I was healthy and had no impairments that would stop me from doing the job. I gave blood, took a hearing test, and a sight test. I mean, you can't be a police officer if you can't see right or hear right. You have to be alert and healthy.

BK: What is the last step of the interview process?

AS: The last step of the process was my final interview. I met with my background investigator and one of the patrol lieutenants. I was asked if I changed my mind about the job and if I still wanted it. They didn't want to waste any time on me in the police academy if I decided at the end of the process that I didn't want it anymore. I explained to them that I have always wanted to become a police officer. I was congratulated for passing the process and given my start date for the police academy. I thought it was finally all over. It had just begun.

BK: Tell me about the police academy.

AS: The next seven months of the police academy were hell. There were times when I wasn't sure about completing it. I just wanted my regular life back. I didn't care for the discipline every day. There were mornings when I would sit in my car and contemplate not going into the academy. I would sit in my car screaming and yelling profanities. I would always see my friends walking in and say to myself, "Okay one more day won't hurt. I'll quit tomorrow," but I never did quit. I never really wanted to quit. I just wanted my life back. I stayed dedicated, though, and I'm glad I did. When I look back on it, I was getting paid (very well) to learn and work out. I mean, who doesn't want that?

A basic day of the police academy consists of two to three hours of defensive tactics and physical training (control holds, take downs, ground fighting, running, push ups, sit ups, weight training). The rest of the day is tests, studying, lectures, guest speakers, etc. There are written and practical tests every week.

Most people go into the police academy in average shape. You have to be in excellent shape prior to the start of the police academy. You can't go into the police academy and hope that it will get you in shape. As long as you're in good shape, that's one less thing you have to worry about in the police academy. I promise there will be a lot to worry about in the police academy. Actually, your entire life is turned upside down while in the police academy.

Everything was worth it in the end. If you can, be single (no relationships) prior to the police academy. Don't worry about going out and partying because most of your nights will consist of studying, training, eating, and sleeping. Plus, you don't want to get in trouble or get caught up with something inappropriate while you're in the police academy.

BK: What did you have to do next?

AS: After I completed the police academy, I had to complete the FTO (Field Training Officer) program. This is when a senior officer rides in the same car with you for twelve to sixteen weeks and makes sure you are doing everything right. The police academy is a controlled environment. The outside world is not a controlled environment. Most police officers say the FTO program is more stressful and difficult than the police academy. I would agree with that. I mean, you can kind of blend in at the police academy. During the FTO program, it's just you and him/her in the car. From using your turn signal to adding a comma in your report, you're scrutinized on everything. You're under the microscope during FTO. You have to focus and understand how much you'll benefit once it's all over.

BK: How long have you been a police officer for?

AS: I've been a police officer for four years. I wouldn't change anything about my life. I love being a police officer, and furthermore, I feel that I'm giving back to the community and helping people out. When you find that feeling, you have to stick with it. It's the best feeling in the world.

The Human Resources Manager

Milaly Tokhi Kaifi was born in Kandahar, Afghanistan, and grew up in San Jose, California. She has been a Human Resources Professional in the Silicon Valley for companies like Cyprus Semiconductor, Globalstar Telecommunications, and Kaiser Permanente. She holds a B.S. in Business Administration with a concentration in Human Resources Management from San Jose State University.

BK: Tell me about your educational journey.

MK: I graduated with an undergraduate degree from San Jose State University in 2000. Looking back, I realize that I graduated at a great time, a time when the job market was at its best and Silicon Valley was booming. New graduates had no problem finding a job. In fact, the employers came to us searching for new and raw talent. I can recall attending many job fairs at San Jose State. It actually got you really excited about your career because of the opportunities that were available.

BK: How did you decide on your major?

MK: I started off declaring Business Administration as my major but was not quite sure of the area of concentration. I knew my interest was in Business Administration, but had to find out in what area of Business Administration I was most interested. I selected "Management" at the time because I was unsure. I was not certain of my choice because there was no clear picture of what I was going to do in Management as far as my career. I thought maybe one day I could be a big time CEO at some well known company, own a franchise, or start my own business, but I still was not content with my decision. As a result, I decided to speak to an advisor and see what he would suggest. The advisor recommended that I take a career oriented class which was an elective course students took to discover their field of interest. I took his advice and attended the course. I found out that there were many personality questionnaires that would help in the decision process. The class was interesting, but I found that it really did not help me much. I went to go see my Business Administration advisor again, and while I was waiting for him, I came across some brief information about each concentration in Business Administration, and that's when I came across Human Resources (HR) Management.

I got really excited because I thought I may have found an area of interest. I spoke to my advisor about it, and he asked me to take some elective courses that focus on Human Resources Management before I switched my concentration from Management to Human Resources Management. That's exactly what I did. I took an Employment Law class along with a Human Resources Labor Law class, and I was thrilled. It was a wonderful feeling to finally land in an area that had caught so much of my interest.

BK: How did you get experience in your field?

MK: I was one year away from graduating and realized I needed to get some hands on experience in my field. All those years of attending the job fairs at San Jose State helped me realize the importance of practical experience. I vividly recall how the professional recruiters at the job fairs emphasized the importance of getting an internship. They told me it did not matter whether it was a paid internship, as long as I got some work experience in my field. They explained that a degree in HR along with an internship under my belt would help me become more competitive. Attending all of those job fairs was not really to land my dream job right away but to gather information from professionals in my field that would eventually better prepare me. I am very grateful for that. I also found out about a very important center that San Jose State offered at the time. It was the Career Building Center. I went there and found a list of jobs posted to which anyone could apply and the majority of those jobs were internships for students. You could also post your resume online for employers to view. The employees of the Career Building Center were mostly students themselves and would help their peers with resume development. After going to the Career Building Center every day and applying to numerous positions to which I had sent my resume, I was able to finally land an internship that I had been waiting for. I was hired as a Human Resources Generalist Intern by a company that specialized in satellite communications. That was the best experience ever, and it opened up many doors.

BK: What characteristics are needed to be successful in the field of Human Resources?

MK: In order to be successful in the field of Human Resources, a person must enjoy working with others by helping them solve their problems within the organization. You have to be able to motivate ordinary individuals with ordinary skills to achieve amazing results. Based upon my experiences, when the people of an organization are happy, the morale goes up along with productivity levels, and in return, a company does well, which keeps everyone's job safe and secure.

BK: What did you do in high school to prepare for college?

MK: There is not much I did personally to prepare for a HR position in high school. What I strongly advise high school students to do is try to find out if your school offers some type of a career planning or building class to take. These types of courses help you early on to figure out where your interests are and what type of person you are.

BK: How long does it take to complete a degree in Human Resources Management?

MK: It should take about four to five years to complete the requirements for a degree in Human Resources Management. As far as becoming a HR Specialist it will take you a good four to five years of work experience. Your college GPA is important if you want to continue to graduate school.

BK: What were some of the challenging courses that you had to take?

MK: As an undergraduate, I faced a few challenging courses, particularly in math. I was able to see a tutor for assistance. I also developed a good relationship with all of my professors and found out when their office hours were so I could communicate with them on a regular basis if I had any questions or concerns. You would be surprised with how happy they are to be of any assistance to you outside of the classroom. The professors with whom I had the closest relationships, were the ones I visited during their office hours. They knew I was eager to learn and pass with a high grade in their class, which pleased them very much. Another strategy I strongly suggest is forming a study group in most of your classes. You would be amazed at how much you can learn from your fellow classmates.

BK: What advice would you give to a student who is considering Human Resources Management as a major?

MK: My advice would be that if you are looking for a high-salary position right away in this field you will be disappointed. It takes a lot of work experience, time, and dedication to become an HR Specialist or a Vice President of HR. My experiences proved that hard work pays off.

BK: What is a typical day like as an HR Specialist?

MK: A typical day at work, as an HR Specialist consists of a variety of tasks. There are many different parts to HR: Recruitment, Staffing Coordinator, Generalist, Benefits Expert, Employee Relations,

HR Business Partner, and many others depending on the organization for which you work. My area of expertise is mostly in recruitment and staffing. I am given a list of vacant positions in my organization, and I am in charge of finding qualified candidates for our hiring managers. It is important to develop a good relationship with each hiring manager because they play a key role in the success of your job.

Each hiring manager performs their job differently and all have different personalities. You have to study and understand each manager if you want your vacant positions filled. This means making frequent trips out to meet the hiring managers in person, finding out what their needs are, learning more about how they run their department, and meeting their staff to see what types of people work for them. It is up to me to do my homework before jumping into filling my vacant jobs. I attend many professional and college recruiting events. I enjoy this part of my job very much. I take pride in my work because I know I am making a positive difference in someone's life. I understand that I am the first point of contact that people will have with the company, and I want it to be pleasant, one that they will never forget. Your role as an HR Specialist really does have a domino effect in the company, and it's up to you to decide in which direction you want the dominoes to land.

The Professor

Marina Aminy was born in Kabul, Afghanistan, and grew up in the San Francisco, Bay Area of California. She completed her B.A. in English, and later her M.A. and Ph.D. degrees in Education, all at UC Berkeley. She is currently a full time English professor at a community college in Southern California. Her professional interests include language development, literacy theory, teacher education, and issues surrounding immigrant and interfaith communities.

BK: Tell me about your journey.

MA: Growing up in the diaspora of an immigrant family, I often found myself confused about my identity. Was I an Afghan or an American? At home I spoke Farsi with my family, and at school I spoke exclusively in English, which came very easily for me, having acquired the language at an earlier age than some of my peers. While I recognized that many of my Afghan peers struggled in school, earning poor grades, and unable to overcome language-learning challenges, I found school to be one of the few stable and dependable areas of my life over which I had control. I dedicated hours to my homework, studying for the SAT exam, and writing and re-writing my personal statements for college applications. Because of our traditional values, my parents insisted that I stay home for college, which meant I would only apply to schools within a 20-mile radius. I aimed for UC Berkeley, and in the spring of my senior year in high school, I received my acceptance letter.

BK: Tell me about your experiences in college.

MA: When I started my freshman year at UC Berkeley, I was torn. On the one hand, I knew I wanted to major in English; it was a natural extension of my interests and abilities. On the other hand, my immigrant background dictated that I should choose a field with more economic and social status, such as engineering or the medical field. My older brother was well on his way earning his degree in civil engineering. Initially, this internal conflict led me to pursue a degree in integrative biology. I took multiple courses in calculus, chemistry, biology (where I was traumatized by the experience of having to dissect a still-warm rat) and even the dreaded organic chemistry course. All along, I was also taking courses in literature, learning about Chaucer, Milton, Thoreau, and other interesting movements and genres of literature. It took me until my third year of college to realize that I was miserable in my science courses, and that I intensely disliked writing lab reports; it paled in comparison to writing a good argumentative essay.

When I finally declared English as my major, it was bittersweet: I was finally taking the upper division courses that I loved, but I was semi-embarrassed by the lack of status in my major. I remember cringing when my mom explained that I was studying English to one of her friends and the Afghan friend asked, "What? Why is she still taking ESL after all this time?"

Beyond my coursework and major, I enjoyed my undergraduate experience at UC Berkley immensely; it was a time in my life when I learned about social justice, history, activism, and politics. The student communities there are incredibly intelligent and active in furthering various causes. I learned about the world and surprisingly, about myself.

BK: How did you transition from a teacher to a professor?

MA: Because of good planning, I was able to graduate in four years from college and I found a job just a couple of months later. Three months after graduating from college, I started working full time as an English teacher; teaching students in grades 7-12, while taking credential courses at night at California State University, East Bay. I found the work rewarding and exciting, especially since I was teaching at my own former middle school and high school. I was finally able to share my love of writing and reading with young, open minds. However, after a few years, I began yearning to go back to school again; I wanted to go back to college for another degree, perhaps another opportunity to learn and write.

When I spoke to one of my favorite English professors from UC Berkeley and mentioned my idea to pursue a Ph.D. in English, she strongly advised against it. She suggested that I would never find a job as an English professor because the field is a dead end. With such a strong caution from someone I trusted, I opted to pursue a Ph.D. in Education, which built upon my work as an educator.

My first position as a full time, tenure-track professor was in the field of teacher education, where I taught credential courses and evaluated new teachers. My courses focused on literacy and language development, and I also spent time directing a reading institute.

This positioned me well for my current position, teaching English at a community college.

BK: What sparked your interest in reading and writing?

MA: Thinking back, it is a wonder that I am now an English professor; I did not always enjoy reading. In my early elementary school years, when my teachers would take our class to the library, I would locate the books with pictures. That way I wouldn't need to read all of the boring words. In fifth grade, my older brother, Jamal, nonchalantly tossed a book my way, a Nancy Drew mystery book, *The Clue of the Broken Locket.* He told me it was a "girlie" book, but that it was "pretty good" and I should read it. Since my big brother was my hero, I immediately set out to read my very first chapter book, with no illustrations. I so enjoyed the story of the brave and brilliant young girl with a tragic past (she had lost her mother) that I read all 12 of the Nancy Drew books in our school library that year. Soon after, I worked out an arrangement with our librarian to let me clean out the library and put up chairs so that I could have first dibs on the next book from the series to arrive at the school. In retrospect, I suspect that she was ordering the books for the library solely to further fuel my interests in reading.

From there, I moved on to reading dozens of other books, including all of Stephen King's horror novels, all of Shakespeare's plays, anything written by the Bronte sisters and well, the rest as you might say, was history. I loved to read and conversely, I loved to write. Crafting a good essay was exciting for me and I felt a sense of utter satisfaction in completing a long paper for my English teachers in high school. And, I found that I was actually good at it; from my years of voracious reading, my comprehension, vocabulary, and grammar skills became well developed.

BK: Tell me about your experiences as a doctoral student.

MA: When I entered the program, again at UC Berkeley, many of my classmates and advisors explained that the *normative* time for completing the program was about seven years, and that many of them had taken up to 10 years to complete the program. However, being a planner, I immediately created a schedule for myself to complete course work, position papers, my comprehensive exam, and dissertation fieldwork. I worked through the coursework and shorter position papers (which were each between 40-50 pages), and when I had collected all of my data, I found myself stuck. With a little support from my advisors and family, I was fortunate enough to be able to dedicate myself completely to graduate school, and finish in four years. It helped that I loved to read and write, and my dissertation was no small task: upon completion, it was about 300 pages of research, literature review, data analysis, and ethnographic methodology. My dissertation, entitled *Constructing the Moral Identity: Language Socialization and Literacy Practices in a Muslim Community* was a culmination of my interests in literacy and education.

BK: Tell me about your career.

MA: Upon graduation from my graduate program, I went on to work part time as a teacher educator at CSU East Bay, teaching new English teachers how to include standards-based instructional practices into their classrooms. I went on to teach at Chapman University and various other schools as *lecturer* or *adjunct* professor (the title most part-time, uncontracted instructors are given).

My first full-time position was as an assistant professor in teacher education at San Jose State University (new professors are called *assistant professors* during the tenure track, which lasts about six years at some universities). The big interview for SJSU was about ten hours long, consisting of a research presentation, several individual interviews, a teaching demonstration, and two meals with the search committee. In my position at SJSU, I worked with new teachers of all content areas (science, math, social studies, and even PE teachers) and helped them to incorporate reading, writing, vocabulary, and other literacy strategies into their courses. So, my work was basically *teaching teachers to teach reading and writing to students.* While I loved my work with new teachers, I confess that I occasionally missed teaching reading and writing directly to my own students.

When I relocated to Southern California, I happily accepted a new position as an English professor at a local community college (our college has a different system for titles, where part time instructors are *associate faculty* and full time instructors are *professors)*. Over the years, my experiences teaching middle school, high school, college, and graduate-level courses had prepared me well for working with college students. I am currently in this position, and enjoying it very much. My English 1B students have recently completed their essays analyzing historical speeches and my English 1A students are working on their thesis papers that examine the causes of a social problem while offering solutions. There will be many exciting successes in my courses this semester, and as always, good organization and planning will be a major part of that journey. Once in a while, I feel a little urge to go back to school, perhaps for another degree, a new skill, another opportunity to learn again. But for now, I am content and grateful to be doing what I love.

BK: What recommendations do you have for others who are interested in following in your footsteps?

MA: When I was asked to share the story of my academic journey, I hesitated to just create a timeline of my academic milestones; real life is not like that, especially when you come from an immigrant background. There were many bumps, discouragements, mentors, prayers, and failures along the way. But through it all, I was fortunate enough to hold on to a few core values:

1. **A little hard work goes a long way:** If you want a good grade in a course, a degree or a job, you have to dedicate hours and hours toward that goal. This often means that you have less time to socialize, party, work (and earn money to buy little luxuries) and even sleep.

2. **Pick your friends:** Surrounding ourselves with like-minded individuals will increase the odds that you will achieve your goals. For example, being a part of a higher-achieving circle of friends in high school meant that we were all aiming high for our college applications, working on our essays, and planning together. I have seen some of my best students become distracted and neglectful of their work because they have friends who are needy of their attention, or who push them toward drugs, alcohol, and other vices.

3. **Be your own advocate**: If you have questions, need help or support, then find that support. There are a lot of people who are open and willing to help you with that essay, college

statement or job interview, but if you do not ask, you will not get help. My most successful students are the ones who come to office hours, who ask questions in class, and who get outside tutoring and support when they need it.

4. **Skip the social scene:** I would strongly caution against becoming too invested in social gatherings and events. The next big party, concert, or picnic requires a lot of time, preparation and money, and if not moderated, your social life will get in the way of your academic goals.

5. **Do not be lured in by shiny coins**: A lot of children of immigrants are tempted to skip college altogether in favor of seemingly high-paying jobs. However, as we have seen, many jobs are often available in "waves" and at the mercy of the economy. While jobs in all sectors suffer in a recession, if you have a college degree, you are more flexible, and it is more likely that you will be able to find another line of work.

6. **Plan, plan, plan:** Take a moment to plan out your life. Ask yourself, "What is it that I would most like to be doing with my career and schooling?" Then, make a five-year calendar for yourself and create some attainable, clear goals. This may involve taking a class, speaking to a counselor, making a decision about a field of study or applying for an internship to start the process. Either way, figure out what you need to do to achieve your immediate and long term goals and start working toward it. It took me years from the time I was in college to when I began teaching English at a college—but everything during those years supported my end goal.

The Pharmacist

Soraia Faizyar was born and raised in the San Francisco, Bay Area of California. She has always loved the art of learning and received her B.S. degree in Biological Sciences, worked on her M.S. in Biology for one year, and received her Pharm.D. degree in May 2010, all from the University of the Pacific. She enjoys helping the community, especially the minorities who are faced with language barriers.

BK: How did you first learn about the role and tasks of a pharmacist?

SF: As I was growing up, I always knew that I wanted to pursue a career in the medical field but never really knew what my niche was. I grew up in a large family surrounded by lots of love but also lots of illness. My father was constantly sick as I was growing up, which forced my older sister and I to quickly learn basic medical terminology and better understand how hospitals operate. Due to the language barrier, my parents sometimes had a difficult time understanding the doctors. As young children, it was also difficult for us to translate, so we relied heavily on our local pharmacist. He was the pharmacy manager at Walgreen's, who eventually became a very close family friend. He understood my need to help take care of my family and to do all that I could when necessary. I remember certain instances when my father's insurance company wouldn't cover a certain medication and our pharmacist would give us an advance on a few pills until the insurance situation would get straightened out. Each time my father was prescribed a new prescription, our pharmacist would make sure that my sister and I understood thoroughly how to administer the medication, what to look out for, and what it was for. He was also very personable and compassionate to my father and his condition, which made him an excellent pharmacist. Being exposed to a whole different world at such a young age inspired me to become a pharmacist.

BK: What made you interested in becoming a pharmacist?

SF: Throughout school, I excelled in science and math courses, and I knew that if I worked hard, I would be a successful health care professional but I just didn't know where my destiny was going to take me. During my senior year of high school, I was assigned a career project so I went to my father for some direction. My father and I were very close and he always motivated me throughout my education. He would challenge me in ways that no one else would. So, I knew that he would be able to provide me with some sense of direction for this project of mine as the deadline was quickly approaching. He said to me, "I know you can do whatever you set your mind to, but have you considered a career in pharmacy?" To be honest, until my father made that suggestion, it had never crossed my mind to even look into that field. But from that moment on, becoming a pharmacist was my primary goal. Although I had a few road blocks along the way, I never gave up because it was my father's dream. I graduated in May 2010, and it was a very bittersweet moment in my life. My father, who was my cheerleader and my motivator, unfortunately passed away due to sudden cardiac complications during my second semester of pharmacy school. After his death, I contemplated whether or not I should pursue this career at all or if I needed to take some time off.

All of my extended family pushed and pushed for me to continue with school, but at that point in my life, I didn't care for it anymore. I sat my mother down one day and told her that I didn't see myself becoming a pharmacist because it hurt so much. With tears in her eyes she looked at me and said, "Your father knew he wasn't going to make it this time around, but he told me to make sure that our daughters completed their education." And so, that is what I did; I fulfilled my father's dying wish. It was such a struggle to go back and pick up where I left off, but I did it. Although my father is not physically present, he is, and will always be in my heart. I owe this journey and success of mine to my hero, my father.

BK: How can a student start preparing for pharmacy school in high school?

SF: Students can begin preparing for pharmacy school as early as high school by developing work experience, participating in extra-curricular activities, and finding mentors in the field. Once a student determines that pharmacy is indeed the right career path for him or her, it is very important to become an active member in the community. There are many different opportunities out there for aspiring pharmacists; it's only a matter of being determined enough to find one that fits one's needs. Young adults can volunteer in the pharmacy, in a hospital or a retail store, and also tutor elementary school students in math and science courses. Applying to college is a very stressful time for all individuals. It may be helpful to make a few visits to the career center at one's high school and to research some of the accelerated pharmacy programs that some schools offer to graduating high school students.

BK: How many years after high school are required to become a pharmacist?

SF: On average it takes about eight to nine years to become a pharmacist. Most pharmacy schools in the nation are now making it a requirement for potential candidates to have completed a B.S. or a B.A. degree prior to applying to pharmacy school.

BK: How important is it for someone to major in a field related to science in college?

SF: It is highly recommended for a potential pharmacist to major in a field related to the sciences but it is not mandatory. I feel as though the individuals who have not majored in a science related field do not have as great of a base knowledge of science compared to those who have majored in a science field. This is not to say that only the individuals who have majored in a science related field are the ones who make good pharmacists; it just makes pharmacy school a little bit easier.

BK: How important is one's GPA in college?

SF: One's college GPA is very crucial. As pharmacy schools become more and more competitive, schools rely on a candidate's GPA as a major part of the application process. This holds true for most careers in the medical field.

BK: As an undergraduate, what were some of your difficult classes?

SF: My hardest year as an undergraduate was my first year. During that time I was taking the first semester of a two series biology class and a chemistry class. It was very difficult juggling a 17 unit class load right out of high school. My lowest grades were in biology and chemistry courses in my freshman year. There were many different factors that played a role in getting my lowest grades. The culprit of this situation was my underestimation of the lab work that came along with each science class. At the time, lab seemed fun and easy, but it really wasn't. Lab was very time-consuming and was a separate class in itself. I wish I would have taken advantage of the interactive learning that took place in those lab classes, but I definitely did learn from this experience in the following semesters.

BK: What exams did you have to take to get into pharmacy school, and how did you prepare for them?

SF: Fortunately for me, I did not have to take any standardized exam to gain acceptance into pharmacy school. I believe that other states besides California require the PCAT, similar to the MCAT, but specialized for pharmacy schools. This is a topic that needs to be addressed by each school, as each school has very individualized requirements.

BK: Describe the pharmacy school interview process.

SF: Each pharmacy school has a different set of requirements. After submitting my application, I was anxiously awaiting an invitation to begin the interview process. Sure enough, I did receive an invitation for an interview. The school had already set out certain Fridays each month for interviews. After setting up the interview, I became obsessed with the student doctor network (www.studentdoctor.net). This is a non-profit organization created to allow students to share their interview experiences from schools all around the nation with one another. I read some blogs of previous students who interviewed with the University of Pacific, and it terrified me. So, until my interview day, I was nervous. The day finally arrived, and I woke up telling myself that I was not going to let my nerves take over my life, and I didn't. Upon arrival, we were addressed by the dean of the pharmacy school and then all of the interviewees were broken into three different groups. One of the groups would begin with the tour of the campus, followed by the interview from a faculty member and a current student, and finally end with a writing sample. The goal of the interview by the faculty member and the current student was for both to get to know the interviewee on a more personal level.

BK: Tell me about your experiences with pharmacy school.

SF: Pharmacy school, especially the program I was in, was very rigorous. My school was year-round and transformed from the traditional three years of didactic experience and one year of rotational experience to two years of didactics and one year of rotational experience. Pharmacy school was very demanding and very competitive, but I learned so much from it all. There was always support from the faculty members and my fellow colleagues, which made it very comforting.

BK: In retrospect, what would you have done differently in pharmacy school?

SF: It is advised in pharmacy school to study a little bit every day as opposed to cramming two weeks before exams or finals. I wish that I would have mastered this because it would have prevented my stress induced ulcers.

BK: What advice or tips would you a give student who is interested in becoming a pharmacist?

SF: I would advise students who are interested in pursuing a career in pharmacy to begin working in a pharmacy as a clerk or a technician early on in their educational career. There are many advantages to this. For example, you are able to witness the role of a pharmacist on a day to day basis, and you become familiar with a lot of the medications, which makes a few classes in pharmacy school easier. There are many different areas of healthcare in which a pharmacist can be involved, and with early experience, it helps solidify your intended area of expertise.

BK: Please tell me about a typical day at work.

SF: As a retail pharmacist, a typical day is spent overseeing all prescription orders that come in and out of the pharmacy. Once a prescription is brought into the pharmacy, it is the duty of the pharmacist to verify that the medication, along with the indication of use and the dose, is appropriate for the patient. If there is any sort of question in regards to what the doctor has prescribed, the pharmacist verifies the information over the phone with the doctor. Ordering medication and making sure that there is enough on the shelves to serve the customers is also in the job duties of a retail pharmacist. Besides being responsible for prescription medications, we are also responsible for over-the-counter medications that we recommend to patients based on symptoms presented. Based on the specialty one goes into, job duties and a typical day can be different.

The School Counselor and Marriage Family Therapist

Wajma Aslami was born and raised in the San Francisco, Bay Area of California. She graduated with a master's degree in Counseling from Saint Mary's College of California where she also earned credentials in Marriage and Family Therapy and School Counseling.

BK: What made you decide to become a School Counselor and Marriage and Family Therapist?

WA: I started college majoring in Biology with the goal of going to medical school. It wasn't until my third year of college when I realized the educational path I was following was not the right one for me; I had absolutely no interest in what I was doing. Shortly after starting my third year as an undergraduate student I took it upon myself to discover what I truly wanted to do and what I expected of my future. I found myself really interested in psychology. After recognizing how fascinated I was, I changed my major and started looking into how I could add to or use the body of knowledge within psychology for my educational and career purposes.

I immediately started doing my own research to see what was available to me. Asking questions of those who were already in the field of psychology really helped to answer a lot of my questions. I found myself very interested in Counseling/Clinical and Educational Psychology. To make sure it was what I really wanted, I shadowed and did volunteer school counseling and field work. I worked side by side with counselors at my former high school. The counselors were very helpful and wanted to make sure I understood their duties clearly. They let me observe them during a typical day to learn more about their responsibilities. I enjoyed and loved being in that environment and still do. Being able to give advice, help students, and make a difference is a satisfying and rewarding feeling that made me want to continue what I was doing and pursue a Master's Degree in Counseling with an emphasis in PPS (Pupil Personnel Services for School Counseling) and MFT (Marriage and Family Therapy).

BK: What characteristics are needed to become a School Counselor/Marriage and Family Therapist?

WA: An individual has to care for the well being of others, be genuine, and non-judgmental. Further, he or she has to have a lot of patience and empathy. It is also important for a school counselor to be culturally aware and understanding of others. Because of the type of work a school counselor and marriage and family therapist does, it is also important to be able to care for oneself.

BK: How many years after high school are required to become a School Counselor and also Marriage and Family Therapist?

WA: It typically takes six years after high school. Four years of college (undergraduate) and an additional two years of graduate school.

BK: How important is one's GPA in college?

WA: If a student is looking to get further education after college, regardless of what major or field, it is important to have a good GPA (3.5 and higher). There are schools that may conditionally accept one if his or her GPA is lower, but in order to have a good chance of getting into a master's program, a 3.5 or higher is typically considered "good".

BK: As an undergraduate, what were some of your difficult classes?

WA: Some of my classes as an undergraduate that required a lot of time and hard work were psychopharmacology, physiological psychology, research statistics, and my labs. Psychopharmacology dealt a lot with learning about the brain and how it functions. I spent a lot of time learning how certain parts of the brain react to certain medications. Physiological psychology is similar to anatomy and physiology but also includes the psychological aspects of why things in our bodies happen the way they do. The research statistics class was very intense. We would do a lot of quantitative research and then analyze our findings and write a report. It was important to learn statistics very well in order to understand what analysis would best work for the type of research that was being done. Lastly, the labs required a lot of time. Each student had to design a study, get it approved, find participants, and follow through with the study that was designed to collect data. Then the data had to be analyzed, and we had to write a report. I had to take three lab classes at once not including the other classes I was required to take.

BK: What exams did you have to take to get into your program?

WA: I had to take the GRE and the CBEST (California Basic Educational Skills Test). The GRE like any other test, requires a lot of studying. I purchased prep books for additional assistance. When preparing for the exam, I would recommend for a student to study a couple of hours a week instead of cramming for it.

The CBEST is a basic test required for school counselors. It has a math, reading, and writing section. There is a prep book for this test as well, however, it is testing for basic information and a college graduate has to do very little preparing for the test.

BK: Describe the interview process.

WA: Each student was required to have an interview. Typically, the interviewer is looking at one's intentions in applying to the program and the expectations one has from the program. Also, it is important to make sure that students are mentally stable and are motivated.

BK: Tell me about your experiences with the school counseling program.

WA: I really enjoyed the program that I was in. It was diverse and the professors were really helpful, understanding, and culturally aware. It is important to be in a program that you will enjoy and one where you will actually learn.

BK: Tell me about your experiences with your field experience/internship.

WA: Before one can start an internship for the PPS credential, one has to get CTC (Commission on Teacher Credentialing) clearance. This means that one will have to apply for clearance with the CTC, take a test of morality, and also get fingerprinted.

I was required to do two different internships within the same year. I had to interview for each internship as if I were interviewing for a job. Each internship required 600 hours, including an internship at two different levels (elementary, middle, and/or high school) for my PPS credential. I did my primary internship at a high school where I completed 400 hours, and I did my secondary internship at a junior high school for my additional 200 hours.

I was also able to complete my MFT hours at the schools where I was working (double counting of hours). The difference is that I had to have a lot of one-on-one time in order to complete the hours. There are very specific requirements when it comes to what can be considered as field experience time. It is important to be very specific and write everything down because it is possible the BBS (Board of Behavioral Sciences) will not approve your hours. For a MFT, the hours, supervisor, and the rest of the requirements are very detailed and specific. Each state has different requirements, rules, and regulations for each credential.

BK: Please tell me about a typical day at work.

WA: At work, I attend faculty, IEP (Individualized Education Programs), and student academic conferences where we discuss academic goals. I go over transcripts with students, help plan future college goals, and advise students on fields of interest. I also have one-on-one meetings with students who are experiencing difficulties at home or school, going through a crisis, or grieving. We also go over student discipline issues, intervention techniques, and effective classroom management strategies with teachers

BK: Is there an exam or thesis to take at the conclusion of the master's program?

WA: There is a thesis that I was required to complete. I had to pick a chair/advisor, and go over possible topics that I came up with. My topic had to be approved by my chair. I was then required to start writing on my own. After all four chapters were completed, my chair and second reader both read it and gave a final approval.

BK: Any additional information that you feel is necessary to include?

WA: A student cannot procrastinate in graduate school. Students should start their thesis in their first semester and not wait until the last minute to start it.

The Software Engineer

Ahmad Khalid Kaifi was born in Kabul, Afghanistan, and is currently a Senior Software Architect in the San Francisco, Bay Area of California. Along with developing enterprise software, he leads a team of Software Engineers specializing in Java, .NET, PHP, Ruby on Rails, software and web application development. He holds a B.S. in Computer Science.

BK: What characteristics are needed to become a successful software engineer?

AK: I believe great software engineers should have a strong foundation in mathematics. To become a software engineer one should major in Computer Science - the study of algorithms, which are processes for solving problems. Having strong analytical skills helps in the design of algorithms to solve real world problems. Another extremely important characteristic of successful software engineers is the ability to communicate complex technical issues clearly and effectively. Being able to write great software is an important ability you will learn throughout your Computer Science program; unfortunately, school does not emphasize the importance of working in teams and communication with your peers. In the workplace, you will most likely work with a team of engineers to develop software. Even the most challenging programming projects will be divided amongst you and your team, so everyone can contribute to complex development and solutions. Being able to work and communicate effectively with your team is crucial to meeting deadlines.

BK: How can a student start preparing for software engineering in high school?

AK: Take all the programming classes your school offers and try to complete math courses up to Calculus. If your school does not offer programming classes, try enrolling in a community college class. Also, spend time on the internet learning a fun web scripting language like PHP.

BK: How many years after high school are required to become a software engineer?

AK: Four. More education is always helpful, but if you continue with school because you are having a hard time finding a job, you should really focus more on your interviewing skills and projects that can showcase your programming abilities, which will give you more to talk about in interviews.

BK: What is the difference between majors in CS and CIS/MIS?

AK: CS, Computer Science, is the study of algorithms, the ability to solve a problem using specific rules in a finite number of steps. Algorithms are created using programming languages that can be compiled into all types of software to help you, businesses, scientists, and servers create, describe, and transform information. CIS/MIS [Computer Information Systems/Management Information Systems] is the study and implementation of software systems to improve business processes. For example, a CIS/MIS graduate could work as an internal IT Consultant for his or her company, finding and implementing software systems to help lower costs. Realistically, in terms of technical hands-on work CIS/MIS graduates would never develop software. Maybe at most, they would maintain software systems as administrators.

BK: How important is one's GPA in college?

AK: Having a good GPA is great, but not very crucial to becoming a good software developer. In the real world, we have the help of debuggers, testers, and all types of resources to produce great quality software. Sitting over a test and having to write pages of code is not always easy and not realistic at all. If you would like to progress to graduate school, then your GPA would be important.

BK: As an undergraduate, what were some of your difficult classes?

AK: All my math courses were difficult: Calculus I, II, III, Discrete Mathematics, Linear Algebra, Differential Equations, Statistical Inference, Numerical Analysis, Analysis of Algorithms, and Theory of Automata. Operating Systems was a difficult class initially, but as the semester went on, I began to grasp concepts much more easily.

Because I was a Computer Science major, I was very focused on my CS and math courses; therefore, I don't remember struggling with anything as much as the long nights working on projects and homework. Personally, non-CS/Math courses were more difficult for me.

BK: In retrospect, what would you have done differently in regards to coursework, exams, and experience?

AK: I would have taken additional programming intensive courses that strongly emphasize the processes related to computer science. You will always look back and remember triumphs from tough courses. Based upon my experiences, my number one piece of advice for a Computer Science major is to complete one or more internships. Work for free, pay your employer, do what you must to get a few years of experience writing code outside of the computer lab and dorm room. This is absolutely crucial.

BK: What advice or tips would you give a student who is interested in becoming a software engineer?

AK: Attend a school that teaches introductory Computer Science in either C or C++, not Java; you will learn memory management and reap the benefits of knowing how to create better and faster algorithms. Don't enter the field because you enjoy playing video games, I think that's a huge misconception. You will learn how to program games, but that is very different from playing games. Don't become a software engineer because you "like" the internet. It's a world of difference. Don't do it because you've built a website before. Building a web site in HTML is just fancy word processing; writing multi-threaded JRuby code that needs to deliver mission critical data is extremely different. Make sure you have a strong mathematical foundation; the best software engineers I have met have always had strong analytical skills.

BK: Please write about a typical day at work.

AK: As a manager and lead architect, my days are spent in meetings with other members of management and executives to make sure the proper decisions are made, so that mission critical data is properly delivered. I design all new software or versions, and then pass their development to senior software engineers working in my department. A typical new graduate starting as a junior software engineer will spend most of his or her early career testing, implementing fixes in codes, or receiving direction from a senior software engineer. Very rarely will a new software engineer actually build something from scratch. I believe that may also be a common misconception of graduates. Typically, you will be working on smaller parts of large software systems with specific guidance by a senior lead.

BK: Please explain some of your projects.

AK: Currently I am the lead architect for 50 different software applications, several of the larger critical applications being:

- The Patient Scheduling System for two Medical Centers.
- The Physician Education system, used by 7000+ physicians and several hundred credentialing staff.
- Employee Compliance Database tracking thousands of employees.
- Online Training, Compliance, and Testing system.
- Surgery Scheduling - Outpatient Surgery Scheduling.
- Close to 45 department-specific applications deployed through desktop and web interfaces.

BK: Do you wish to add any additional information that you feel is necessary to include?

AK: I highly recommend all Computer Science majors to read the following books before graduation:

- *Code Complete 2* by Steve McConnell
- *The Pragmatic Programmer* by Andrew Hunt and David Thomas
- *The Mythical Man-Month* by Fred Brooks
- *Design Patterns: Elements of Reusable Object-Oriented Software* by Erich Gamma, Richard Helm, Ralph Johnson, and John Vlissides
- *The Art of Computer Programming* by Donald Knuth

Also, learn how to read other people's code; this skill alone will help you vastly improve your own programming skills and progress in your future place of employment. Write code that other people can read and comment upon, regardless of how much you believe your code is "self-documenting" and precise. You should love writing code and tackling difficult, if not impossible projects. Lastly, and most importantly, learn to listen, speak, and write very clearly. I personally believe that my greatest skill as an effective software developer has been my ability to communicate rather difficult technical issues clearly, precisely, and effectively to non-technical managers and executives.

The Registered Nurse

Maira Noori Wardak was born in Kabul, Afghanistan. She grew up in Sacramento, California. She completed her B.S. in Nursing at Dominican University of California in San Rafael. She is currently employed as a Nurse in a fast-paced Emergency Room in Oakland, California, where she works primarily with low-income and underserved populations.

BK: What made you decide to become a registered nurse?

MW: When I was in my last year of high school, my father asked me to seriously begin thinking about my future and the lifestyle I wanted for myself. At that point of my life, I was uncertain about the direction I was going to take in academics. I thought about becoming a psychiatrist, a businesswoman, or even a doctor. My father asked me to do some research about registered nursing (RN). Sure enough, I found many "pros" in this career and knew that this was what I wanted to do. I was not interested in spending a lot of time in school, but I wanted financial stability, job security, a noble career, personal gratification, flexible scheduling, and the ability to work in other countries. Registered nursing gave me all of this.

BK: What characteristics are needed to become a successful registered nurse?

MW: I feel that the number one characteristic is the love for helping others. This does not stop at the patient; it also involves the family. Being in the hospital, whether you're the patient or the family member, can be very stressful; therefore, the RN must have patience in helping others to reduce their stress. This can be done by answering questions, explaining procedures, and constantly updating the patient and family. Other important characteristics are critical thinking, multi-tasking, and prioritizing. These three go hand-in-hand. The hospital can be chaotic at times, and it's crucial to remain calm and to prioritize the tasks at hand.

BK: How can a student start preparing for nursing school in high school? What subject(s) should a person focus on?

MW: A student in high school can start preparing for nursing school by taking classes such as anatomy, physiology, psychology, chemistry, and statistics. Start volunteering at the local hospital and interview a registered nurse. Give yourself time to study for the SAT/ACT exams since most universities take these scores into consideration along with volunteer hours. Ask for letters of recommendation from your teachers and volunteer coordinator. Last, but not least, visit and interview different nursing programs.

BK: How many years after high school is required to become a registered nurse?

MW: The number of years it takes to become a registered nurse depends on whether one wants to apply to a certificate program or a BSN program. The certificate program requires at least two years of full time study while the BSN program can take as long as four and a half years.

BK: What is the difference between someone who has a BSN versus an RN?

MW: Besides the difference in the length of the program, there is a difference in the curriculum and the future for advancement. Upon completion of a BSN program, one receives a Bachelor of Science in Nursing. An RN program is offered at community colleges, where an associate degree in registered nursing can be obtained. Also, trade schools offer certificates in nursing. Both BSN and RN programs have the same core concepts and clinical experience but the BSN includes theory and research along with other upper division classes. Generally, licensed graduates of any of the three types of educational programs qualify for entry-level positions as staff nurses. The BSN program, however, offers more opportunities for advancement such as becoming a charge nurse or a nurse manager. Some hospitals will give a pay increase for a BSN, and some require it in order to work in certain specialty areas such as critical care and emergency services.

BK: What is the difference between a CNA, LVN, and RN?

MW: A certified nurse's assistant (CNA) is usually a six to twelve week program. Under the supervision of an RN, the job requirements are limited to basic care services such as bathing, grooming, feeding, assisting nurses with medical equipment, checking patients' vital signs, and providing vital information to nurses.

A licensed vocational nurse (LVN) is an eleven month full-time program in California. An LVN must be supervised under an RN or doctor and cannot do everything that an RN does. In most states, a LVN cannot start an intravenous line (IV) but can take blood. A LVN cannot administer IV medication, assess a patient, or give discharge instructions.

Registered nurses, regardless of specialty or work setting, treat patients, educate patients and the public about various medical conditions, and provide advice and emotional support to patients' family members. They record patients' medical histories and symptoms, help perform diagnostic tests and analyze results, operate medical machinery, administer treatment and medications, and help with patient follow-up and rehabilitation.

Registered nurses teach patients and their families how to manage their illnesses or injuries, explain post-treatment home care needs such as diet, nutrition, and exercise programs, and self-administration of medication and physical therapy. Some registered nurses may work to promote general health by educating the public on warning signs and symptoms of diseases. They also might run general health screening or immunization clinics, blood drives, and public seminars on various conditions.

BK: How important is one's GPA in high school and nursing school?

MW: Both high school and nursing school GPA's are very important. Nursing programs are competitive and acceptance is based on high school GPA, letters of recommendation, community service, and experience. A high GPA in a BSN program is crucial when applying to a Master of Science in Nursing (MSN) program. Also, if a RN would like to apply to a bridge program for a BSN degree, experience and a high GPA along with letters of recommendation are required.

BK: What classes or exams did you have to take to get into nursing school?

MW: I took the ACT test and prerequisites required for the nursing program. My classes included anatomy, physiology, organic and inorganic chemistry, microbiology, statistics, psychology, sociology, food and nutrition, life span development, and pharmacology, along with general education classes.

The only way to prepare for each class is to set time aside for studying, take accurate notes, attend class religiously, set up study groups, read the required material before class, and prepare a list of questions or clarifications one may have for the professor.

Some of the requirements to apply to a BSN program have since changed and not all schools have the same requirements. I recommend further research on the student's part.

BK: Describe the nursing school interview process.

MW: The school I attended did not require an interview. Acceptance was based on GPA, letters of recommendation, community service, ACT score, and an entrance essay.

BK: Tell me about your experiences in nursing school.

MW: I had a wonderful experience, and I believe my school's location and size had a great deal to do with this. I received one-on-one attention from my professors who all knew me by name. My school has a great reputation for its nursing program at the surrounding hospitals, so we received top priority for clinical locations. Although it was hard and stressful at times, I enjoyed being challenged on a daily basis.

BK: Can someone have a specialty in nursing?

MW: Nursing has many specialties; this is also one of the many things that drew me to my career. The ideal specialty has a great deal to do with one's personality. For example, I like not knowing what might come through the door and the organized chaos that exists in the emergency room. The emergency room offers a little bit of everything, from "flu-like symptoms" to heart attacks and gunshot wounds. Nursing students are provided opportunities to explore different specialties through clinicals associated with certain courses. I recommend researching the areas that are not covered in clinicals, visiting those departments, and interviewing nurses in those specialties.

BK: What exam did you have to pass to become a nurse? How long was the exam?

MW: Before one can become a registered nurse, he or she has to pass the National Council Licensure Examination (NCLEX). The NCLEX is a computerized adaptive test, also known as a tailored test that adapts to the examinee's ability level. The test can be anywhere from 75 questions to 260 questions with a time limit of six hours. The majority of test items are written at the application or higher levels of cognition but the exam may include items at all of the cognitive levels; mainly, memorization or recalling, knowledge, analysis, and application.

BK: In retrospect, what would you have done differently in regards to coursework, exams, and experience?

MW: The only thing I would have done differently is attend school full time from the very beginning and not waste time with working and being a part time student.

BK: What advice or tips would you give a student who is interested in becoming a registered nurse?

MW: Work hard from the very beginning and do not waste time. Find out what schools you are interested in and what their requirements and deadlines are. Keep in mind that the better your grades are and the more community service you do, the better your chances are in getting into the school of your choice. If you receive an acceptance letter from a nursing school, even if it is not your first choice, register into that program because this opportunity may not come around again. Talk to as many nurses as you can. Make sure that nursing is your passion, as it is not an easy road and takes dedication.

BK: Please write about a typical day at work.

MW: A typical day starts with a huddle where the charge nurse gives us a briefing of how the day has been going and updates the staff on new policies or procedures. Next, the charge nurse assigns me to take over for a nurse that is leaving for the day. The nurse will give me a report on the patients that are under his or her care. After I take a quick look at his or her nursing notes and the doctor's orders, I prioritize which patient I see first based on the information that I received. I visit the patients, introduce myself, and update them on their status. After I discharge, transfer, or admit patients, I receive a new patient from the waiting room or from an ambulance. Sometimes, I pick up my own patients and sometimes the charge nurse will assign them to me. I can have a maximum of four patients if their acuity level is not high. If I have critical patients then I am required to only have two patients under my care. We have standing orders depending on the chief complaint of the patient, which serve as guidelines and do not require a doctor's order. These standing orders can include lab work, IV, IV fluids, EKGs, diagnostics tests, and certain medications. Emergency nursing allows for a great deal of autonomy. When my twelve hours are over, I provide a report to the next nurse.

The Lawyer

Aref Wardak was born in Kabul, Afghanistan, and grew up in Oakland and Stockton, California. He received a B.S. in Neuroscience and Physiology and a B.A. in Psychology from UC San Diego, followed by an M.P.A. from the University of Southern California, and a J.D. from the University of Michigan. He currently practices corporate law with a focus on venture capital, mergers and acquisitions, and securities. He also dedicates significant time to pro bono legal work on behalf of organizations serving refugees, victims of domestic violence, and urban youth.

BK: What made you decide to become a lawyer?

AW: It started with a process of elimination. I was initially attracted to medicine but after spending hundreds of hours volunteering in hospitals, sitting in on medical school classes, and shadowing doctors in mentorship programs, I came to realize medicine was not for me. I then explored a future in academia and research. I double majored in neuroscience/physiology and psychology so I was naturally attracted to the cognitive sciences. I worked in a lab and interned at another. As with medicine, I came to realize pure research and academia was not for me.

Given the long line of public servants on both sides of my family, my "second-choice" had always been a life of civil service. After my undergraduate degree, I received a Master's in Public Administration and worked in education finance and policy and judicial administration. Through the course of my work experience, I came to realize that at any pivotal moment in addressing certain matters of policy, it was always the lawyers in the room whose words carried the greatest weight. I explored the field of law further and my findings cemented my desire to attend law school.

BK: What characteristics are needed to become a successful lawyer?

AW: This really depends on the type of law one practices. As for corporate law, an inquisitive and analytical mind is vital for success. It is often simply intellectual curiosity that compels an attorney to delve into convoluted and often arcane legal matters and come up with solutions to a client's dilemma.

BK: How can a student start preparing for law school in high school?

AW: The best preparation would be improving one's reading and writing skills. I would also urge students to become familiar with concepts of logic.

BK: How many years after high school is required to become a lawyer?

AW: Generally, it takes seven years, including the undergraduate years.

BK: How important is it for someone to major in a field related to law in college?

AW: A law-related major is not required. In fact, law-related majors are generally not encouraged by law schools. An evaluation of the undergraduate degree for purposes of admission is primarily concerned with performance and difficulty of the chosen course of study. Undergraduate degrees closely related to law may generally be considered to be lacking intellectual rigor.

In regards to preparation for a career in law, any major that requires critical thinking, analysis, and writing (particularly analytical and persuasive) would be ideal. Areas such as economics, logic (and philosophy in general), and some of the sciences are especially good fits.

BK: How important is one's GPA in college?

AW: The GPA is the second most important factor in the admission process, just behind the LSAT score.

BK: What exam(s) did you have to take to get into law school?

AW: I took the LSAT. While I used a variety of preparation material to help me understand the exam, the most useful part of my preparation was taking practice tests.

There are dozens of older LSATS released to the public. I wrote as many practice exams as I could. When I took the LSAT, the focus of the exam was on reading comprehension and logic. Neither area is especially difficult as tested. If given infinite time, most test-takers would do very well. However, managing to get through all the questions within the provided time-constraint poses a problem for most test-takers. That's where practice exams come in.

BK: Was there a law school interview process.

AW: Some schools, such as Northwestern, require all applicants to participate in an interview conducted either by the admissions office or alumni. Other schools offer a voluntary interview process to supplement the application. Most schools do not provide for an interview process.

BK: Tell me about your experiences with law school.

AW: Law school presented my favorite academic experience. It was an opportunity to engage with incredibly bright students and faculty from across the world. I was able to take classes with professors who literally "wrote the book" in their fields. It offered a myriad of interesting subject matters to explore ranging from corporate finance to human rights and even Nordic law as practiced by the Vikings. Through law school I was able to work with a human rights organization in London and a Refugee law court in Auckland. I was also able to take classes in international law in Curacao. Law school allowed me to meet incredible people, study interesting matters, and spend several months on three different continents. Of course, it also opened doors for work after graduation.

BK: How does one specialize in a specific area of law?

AW: One can choose a course of study in law school that emphasizes certain areas of law, which is important when choosing a specific type of law versus another (e.g. public interest law vs. corporate law). However, course selection matters less when choosing between sub-specialties such as: securities, bankruptcy, or mergers and acquisitions. In fact, students who are headed for corporate law are often advised to take a variety of courses with the understanding that the specific instruction required to practice a specific area (e.g. bankruptcy, securities, mergers or acquisitions) will occur on the job.

With fewer resources to train, public interest entities often prefer candidates who have extensive coursework in a relevant area.

BK: What is the Bar exam and what does it consist of? How long does it take to complete the exam?

AW: Successfully passing the Bar exam is required in order to practice law in most states and each state has a different Bar exam. The California Bar exam is generally considered the hardest exam and has the lowest passage rate. The California Bar is given over three days (about 8 hours each day including breaks). The exam consists of both multiple choice questions that require knowledge of the State's black letter law and a series of writing exercises.

BK: Why is it better to go to an ABA accredited law school?

AW: ABA accredited law schools generally tend to offer a higher quality education, student body, faculty, and facilities. Further, and perhaps most important, graduating from an unaccredited law school will drastically limit one's career options. While there are opportunities to improve one's professional standing over a lifetime, a lawyer's academic pedigree will remain with him and influence his entire career.

BK: In retrospect, what would you have done differently in regards to coursework, exams, experience, and specialty?

AW: I would have taken more courses related to corporate law. The conventional wisdom at many law schools is that one should take a wide breadth of courses and focus on learning the corporate work on the job. While it's generally true that most of the legal knowledge necessary to practice corporate law is learned on the job, starting a corporate career familiar with some basic concepts and verbiage surely provides a leg up.

BK: What advice or tips would you give a student who is interested in becoming a lawyer?

AW: I would advise young students to get over any sense of insecurity or inferiority they may have as a potential advocate. During law school, I found that many of my Asian and Middle Eastern peers faltered during job interviews as they were unable to fully communicate their virtues. The legal industry and employers, value a confident presence.

BK: Please write about a typical day at work.

AW: Each day varies depending on client needs. Further, unlike most jobs, there is no real start to the day. The firm provides us with laptops and smartphones which allows for a link to the firm's system so we are essentially on the clock 24 hours a day. This is even more relevant when working with international matters. In the mornings, I like to do a quick mental check on where I am on each client matter and review my calendar for any scheduled calls or meetings. I typically have up to seven open matters at any given time.

For example, I started a recent day drafting incorporation documents for a group of entrepreneurs who wanted to form a company in Delaware. I then began drafting various agreements between a group of investors and entrepreneurs. Those agreements required a review of various statutes to make sure we complied with certain SEC (Securities and Exchange Commission) reporting requirements. I then called a pro bono asylum client to follow up and ask a few questions concerning his case. After that call, I got on another call concerning the planned initial public offering of a firm client. It was an introductory call between the client, underwriters, and all the relevant firms involved in the deal. While on that call, I responded to a series of emails regarding the documents I drafted earlier. I also emailed a potential client. After the call, I contacted a paralegal and had her prepare a closing volume for a financing that we completed the week before.

The Global Musician

Salar Nader was born in Hamburg, Germany, and grew up in the San Francisco, Bay Area of California. He completed his B.A. in

Psychology at San Francisco State University. He has been playing the tabla for over 25 years and is a student of Ustad Zakir Hussain.

BK: When did you get your first pair of tablas?

SN: My father purchased my first pair when I was only six months old.

BK: When did you start performing at functions?

SN: At the age of three, I started performing to Afghan folk music.

BK: How important is it to have a great teacher in the music industry?

SN: It is very important. I was very fortunate that I grew up in the Bay Area because one of the most knowledgeable musical teachers of North Indian classical music was living in Marin County, which was about 50 miles away from my house. It was in the summer of 1988 (at the age of seven) when my father took me into Ustad Zakir Hussain's musical course with an emphasis on tabla. That summer course was the official start of my musical journey.

BK: Briefly explain the initiation process in the North Indian classical tradition.

SN: When a student is initiated in the North Indian classical tradition, he or she makes a life-long bond with his or her "Guru" [teacher]. One must commit his or her lifetime to the Guru because the "Guru is the one who removes the darkness" according to the North Indian classical tradition. The sacred tradition is known as the Guru-Shishya-Parampara, literally meaning the teacher-student-tradition. The teacher is responsible for not only teaching the student music, but also helping the student become a better human being. In the older days, a disciple had to live with the Guru and take on daily tasks, cooking, cleaning, and basically becoming the Guru's servant. In return, the Guru would treat the student as a member of the family.

BK: When did you have your official initiation ceremony?

SN: I had my official ceremony at the age of 12 where I was blessed by Ustad Zakir Hussain and Ustad Salamat Ali Khan.

BK: How has Ustad Zakir Hussain helped you throughout the years?

SN: As a young artist in America we try to do as much as we can when possible; obviously we cannot emulate all of the old traditional duties, but many of the same responsibilities are still very important. Ustad Zakir Hussain has guided me in all walks of life. My Ustad is not only my musical teacher, but he is also my mentor, whom I consult with and seek advice from. We have a strong bond that is built upon respect, trust, and passion for music.

BK: What made you decide to become a musician?

SN: Destiny. I started playing and performing at an early age and it was not a decision that I ended up making while performing within the professional music circuit. By the time I was twelve years old, I was performing for many benefit concerts which were related to the development of Afghanistan. My parents always encouraged me to donate my time and money to any organizations which were related to people in need, be it Afghan or non-Afghan people.

BK: How did you decide on the tabla?

SN: Tabla was my calling as a child and it was not a choice. The instrument was a friend who was always there for me no matter what. To sum it up, music was my best friend, my passion, and later on, it became my profession without needing to think twice about it.

BK: How important is raw talent in music?

SN: The majority of success in music is related to the talent and the overall capacity of the individual. Once it is apparent that the child has the potential it is very important that he or she is immediately taken to a knowledgeable instructor.

BK: How can a person start preparing for a musical career?

SN: Take up music courses at a nearby school of music. I think it is very important for a multicultural student to learn both western notation and also the traditional music which is related to his or her country of origin. Having both backgrounds will prepare the student for the future and if he or she is planning on teaching, it will be very nice to fuse the two styles together. This will help the artist become a niche artist and teacher.

BK: How long does it take to become a professional in your field?

SN: Well it really depends on the individual. My Ustad was performing professionally in his late teens and was touring internationally. In our tradition, the Guru will encourage their student to perform at a specific stage in his or her career and that is basically the green light for the student to cautiously start performing. It is equally important to have permission from your Guru by getting blessings upon performance inquiries. As time goes on, the student does not have to do this for every single performance.

BK: How important is time-management?

SN: Time management is a very important part of one's musical career. Those who have great time management skills will have more time to master an instrument.

BK: How many hours of practice would you recommend?

SN: On weekdays a student must put in at least five to six hours of hands on practice. An average day should include three separate times where one will practice their tabla performance and recitation. It is very important for a student to reflect upon each practice session by being able to implement useful corrections so he or she can continuously improve. You have to remember your teacher's advice throughout each practice session. Musicians can spend up to 12-16 hours a day practicing if one includes the hours which are spent teaching, listening, and educating themselves by transcribing performance materials.

BK: What advice would you give a young student who is interested in becoming a musician?

SN: Find the closest musical school available in your area. Be very patient and understand that this is a life-long commitment in one specific area of study.

BK: Who are some of the artists that you have performed with thus far?

SN: Some of the artists that I have performed with so far are: Ustad Salamat Ali khan (vocal), Ustad Sultan khan (sarangi), Ustad Ghulam Ali khan (Urdu ghazal vocal), Ustad Sharafat Ali khan (vocal), Pandit Ajoy Pohankar (vocal), Pandit Ramesh Misra (sarangi), Ustad Habib khan (sitar), Ahmad Wali (Farsi vocal), Ustad Eltaf Hussain, Antonia Minnecola (kathak), Shafqat Ali khan, Pandit Chitresh Das (kathak), Najim Nawabi, Ustad Jalil Zaland, Ustad Farida Mahwash, Ustad Hussain Bakhsh (guloo), Ustad Shahid Parvez (sitar), Ustad Shujaat khan (sitar), Ustad Aashish khan (sarode), Homayun Sakhi (rubab), Alam khan (sarode), Rahul Sharma (santoor), Kala Ramnath (violin), Shahram Nazeri (vocal), Hafez Nazeri (vocal), Hamed Nikpay (vocal), Assal Nasri (vocal), Azam Ali (vocal), Riffat Sultana (vocal), Fareed Haque (guitar), Mala Ganguly (vocal), George Brooks (saxophone), Aziz Herawi (dootar), Cheb Khaled (king of Rai), Naim Popal (vocal), Chebi Sabbah (producer), Dr. Das (bass/producer), Mahesh Kale (vocal), Mel Ryne (jazz), Ustad Bahudeen (tanbur), Ehsan Aman (vocal), Kronos Quartet (classical), Hafez Modirzadeh (saxpohone), and Farzin Farhadi (saxphone).

BK: How did your first visit to India influence your daily practice?

SN: After my first visit to India in 2003, I began a very strict reyaz (practice) regimen for producing clarity of the bols (syllables) and the phrases. In India, due to the artistic environment, I was able to really dive deep into the art and improve my skills. It was an eye-opening experience for me to be among aspiring tabla players and scholarly musicians. The daily practice regime helped improve my delivery.

The School Teacher

Sayed Z. Anwar was born in Kabul, Afghanistan, and grew up in the San Francisco, Bay Area of California. He completed his B.A. in U.S. History at UC San Diego. He is currently a full time History teacher at a Middle School in the Bay Area. His professional interests include the National Geographic Bee, conflict management, and school/community programs.

BK: What made you decide to become a school teacher?

SA: The very short answer is that as a teacher I have the opportunity to make a huge difference in someone's life and hence make a little difference in the world. This doesn't mean that I think I do make a difference, but I know that I have the opportunity. In my past professions, I did not feel like I really made a difference or that I even had that opportunity.

I took a different road than your average teacher to get here. From my experience, most people either become a teacher right out of college or it's something they fall back on as a career; I ended up doing both. Though I went to UC San Diego with every intention of becoming a teacher, I ended up working in the high-tech field (software sales and marketing) after college. Financially, it made more sense for me, considering where teacher salaries start in most public school districts. As a child of refugees in this country, I had to follow the money and make a living for my family first and any personal satisfaction with my career came in second. A decade and four kids after college, I was going through old boxes of my school papers from middle school, and I came across a project that I had from my 7th grade English class. It was a "what do you want to be when you grow up" type of project. After reading what I had written as a 12 year old, I was inspired enough to quit my job the next day and start the credential program at Saint Mary's College.

BK: What characteristics are needed to become a successful school teacher?

SA: I believe that the first characteristic that a successful teacher needs is patience. Anyone who has to deal with children in general has to be a very patient person because, unlike the business world or any other profession, you don't get to see your final product or what impact you have had. You can't just make a child become a better student or a better person in a few classroom sessions or even a year.

Developing children is not the same as developing software. If you are making a product, and it just doesn't work and takes too much time to make, you can quit and either make something else or start over. You can't do that as a teacher; you can't just quit making your product.

The second characteristic that I believe is important to be a successful teacher is knowledge. You have to be knowledgeable about the subject you teach of course, but you also have to be knowledgeable about other subjects as well. As a student, you need your teachers to know more than the average person you run into on the street. As a student it was very hard for me to respect a teacher who was not knowledgeable.

The third characteristic that a teacher needs is to be personable. If you are a timid person socially; or a very shy person, I would not recommend teaching as a profession. I believe that teaching is a relationship and like all other relationships it has to be built on honesty, respect, and kindness. I have to build a relationship with my students, with their parents, and I have to be a part of the community.

I have to get to know who my students are, what they like, where they come from, and what social ills or obstacles are facing them. Like all other relationships in life, the teacher and student relationship will have its ups and downs, and I have to work on it on a regular basis. I have to work on my relationships with my students just like I do with my family; I have to actually work harder on my relationship with my students because I only see them for an hour a day and that becomes my only opportunity to build any sort of bond.

BK: How can a student start preparing for a field in education while in high school?

SA: If a student is interested in the field of education as a profession, he or she should be involved in school as much as possible. The student should be involved in leadership, clubs, and sports to understand how schools function and what roles they play in every student's life and community. They should find teachers whose teaching styles they enjoy and should spend time as a TA (teacher assistant) in the classroom if possible. Not only observing the way a teacher teaches, but grading the lessons and helping set up the class will give a student good exposure to the field of education. The goal of education is to create a well rounded individual, not a single-minded robot.

Every person is born and gifted with certain skills or intellectual strengths. The goal of middle school should be to begin exposing them to different subjects and ideas, so that students can begin seeing beyond themselves. I believe this process continues into high school, and the more exposure a student has to different ideas and subjects, the better prepared he or she will be for a career in any profession. High school should be about teaching students how they impact, relate to, and create the world around them. College is really the time that students should start thinking about a career path based upon the intellectual skills that they are born with. Students might realize that they enjoy chemistry because they not only had a class on the subject, but also enjoyed the labs. They may realize that this is a strength for them, and this may be what they want to dedicate their life to. In college, they may realize that they don't want to spend the rest of their life in a lab, but they do enjoy the outdoors and nature. They can use their strengths toward soil science where they get to be outside and still excel in their chosen field. I believe the most important thing that students need to understand is that their career path (like life) is windy, and you may even have to change roads to reach a successful and fulfilling career destination.

BK: How many years after high school are required to become a school teacher?

SA: You need a four year degree, and you need to finish a teaching credential program. Some universities offer the credential programs that are imbedded into a degree. Other universities offer a teaching credential imbedded into a master's program, so you can finish both at the same time.

BK: What should someone major in if they are interested in becoming a school teacher?

SA: Major in a subject that you are passionate about and one that you would like to spend the rest of your life learning. You should major in the core subjects offered at public schools like Math, Science, English, and History. For example, a student who wants to become a teacher should major in History and not Urban Studies or Sociology.

BK: How important is one's GPA in college?

SA: I believe that in order to be a good teacher you have to be a good student. You should be able to maintain above a 3.0 in college in order to get into some credential programs.

BK: What is the difference between a single subject credential and a multiple subject credential?

SA: A multiple subject credential will authorize an individual to teach any subject from kindergarten through 6th grade. An individual will need to pass the RICA (Reading Instruction Competence Assessment), multiple subject CSET (California Subject Examinations for Teachers), and a U.S. Constitution test to acquire the credential. A single subject credential authorizes an individual to teach one subject that he or she specializes in (grades 7-12). An individual will need to pass a single subject CSET and a U.S. Constitution test, as well.

BK: What exams did you have to take to get into a teaching credential program?

SA: To get into a teaching credential program you need to pass the CBEST. I believe that you should be prepared to take the CBEST if you have a high school diploma. It is not a difficult test to pass (you can start substituting in a classroom as soon as you pass it). The test is on basic algebra, reading comprehension, and writing skills.

BK: Tell me about your experiences with student teaching.

SA: I was a student teacher for a year at two different schools. Unfortunately, it was a negative experience for me. I was not very impressed by the master teachers who were assigned to me. Both of my master teachers did not enjoy what they did for a living, disliked the kids, and were very unhappy people. They had both given up on the teaching profession and their students long before I walked into their classrooms. You have to remember that working with children is just like working with adults; they can be selfish, ungrateful, ignorant, and mean. Teachers should not expect their students to be obedient and respectful because this will burn them out, like it has a lot of teachers with whom I have worked. Teachers should be strong and hopeful that they will teach selflessness, gratitude, wisdom, and kindness along with the subject they teach.

BK: What advice or tips would you give a student who is interested in becoming a school teacher?

SA: My honest advice is to be sure that you have very thick skin. Teaching is not for the meek, and you will have to be a strong person to survive year in and year out. Teaching in America is nothing like teaching in other countries. Teaching in America can seem like a thankless job without any respect, so you really need strong ideals and motivation that will help you keep going. Remember that you are a teacher for all students and not just the good ones, so don't pick favorites. My favorite teachers were the ones who made me feel proud of myself, and I try to do the same for all of my own students. Everyone's cultural pride should be important to you as a teacher.

BK: Please write about a typical day at work.

SA: I get to work between 7am and 7:30am every morning. I am usually available in the mornings to help students with any questions they may have before school begins. This gives me an opportunity to deal with students socially and build on that teacher/student bond before class even begins. School starts at 8:20am, and I have one prep period from 9:00am to 9:45 am. I usually make copies or go over my lesson plans for the day during this time. Lunch is from 11:30 am to 12:00 pm; I spend my lunch with a group of my students who call themselves the 'lunch bunch.' I teach two 8th grade history classes and one 7th grade world history class. School is over at 2:45pm. I have students coming in for tutoring or extra help after school, and they usually stay until 4:30pm. I stay and grade papers until 5pm. I go home with any work that I still have to finish, usually grading, creating lesson plans, building PowerPoint presentations, and communicating with parents. On average, I have about two hours of work after I get home that still needs to be completed.

BK: What kind of a work schedule do you have?

SA: I work 180 days a year with summers off. My schedule gives me time to travel and work on hobbies and other interests. The best perk that comes with the job is that when my children are home from school, so am I, and there are no business trips that take me away from my family overnight.

Summary

This chapter provided useful information by professionals who are currently working in their respected fields. The participants were able to convey their strategies for being successful. The suggestions and recommendations made by each participant will help others who are interested in following in their footsteps.

Chapter Eight Discussion Questions

1. Throughout life, why is it so important to learn from others?
2. What inspires you to strive for excellence?
3. What are your educational goals and how are you going to accomplish them?

4. Which interview was the most interesting to you? Why?
5. How will you give back to others in your community?

CHAPTER 9

Conclusion and Words of Advice

"A person who never made a mistake never tried anything new."
– Albert Einstein

Life is full of decisions that can impact one's future. Anytime a decision is made, there are consequences. There are different ways to make decisions, but the most logical way is to make informed decisions. Making the decision to be educated is one of the most important decisions that an individual will ever make. Education is an investment and the return on investment (ROI) is stability, security, and success. Each day, the value of education increases and those without an education are left behind. Many years ago, a high school diploma was sufficient for obtaining a job that paid well enough to survive. Today, with global competition, a volatile economy, and high unemployment rates, those without a college degree are unable to live a prosperous life. The future may require even higher levels of education for each person in a society. In certain areas of the world, education is considered a luxury and only for the elite whereas in other parts of the world education is a necessity of life. The beauty of education is that it is the one thing in life that no one can take away from anyone else. Money can be taken away, power can be taken away, loved ones can be taken away, and even talent or skill can be taken away. Education will always endure with an individual and will help an individual make decisions that are worthwhile. Being educated will open up many doors that can result in success. Consider the following strategies for success.

Strategies for Success[*]

- Learn to accept yourself. Don't feel that you have to be like someone else, and instead, celebrate the fact that you are different. Whether this difference has to do with economics, ethnicity or race, don't dwell on the past, and remember that the past does not equal the future. Avoid thinking that you should become your ideal self right this second. That ideal is something to work toward for the future and will happen with time. Here, in the present, you are okay. Self-acceptance means learning to believe in your heart that you are valuable, and that your differences from others are more of a plus than a minus. Differences are what make everyone so interesting and unique.

- Develop an internal locus of control. People with an internal locus of control feel that they are in control of events in their own lives and have more of a take-charge attitude. In life, take initiative in all situations. Locus of control is also related to both higher self-esteem and better physical health. On the other hand, people with an *external* locus of control feel that the world is happening to them, and that they have no control over the events in their lives. Be proactive and less reactive.

- Develop a winning skill. If you have a special hobby or interest, spend some time cultivating that skill on a consistent basis. Developing a skill puts focus on your positive qualities and takes focus away from the negative. This adds to your self-efficacy. Also, developing one area will teach you to focus on achievements, which are necessary for growth and having a positive "glass is half full" attitude. Success in one area often spills over into other areas. Finally, you'll begin to feel more self-respect. Don't let a day go by without doing something that you can do very well.

- Study confident people. Study those who seem to have strong self-esteem and learn their positive behaviors. Such behaviors might include ways of dealing with negative responses from other people, daily habits, or even the way they treat others. You do not have to be just like anyone else; in fact, losing your identity can destroy your self-

---

[*] Adapted from: *WCC Antioch Quarterly Newsletter*, Kaifi, B.A. (2010), 1(4), and also *Human Relations*, Lamberton, L., & Minor, L. (2010).

esteem. However, you can learn skills from others that you can apply to your own life and well being.

- *Read biographies of people you admire.* You'll be amazed at how many self-esteem hints you can pick up from a good biography such as Dr. Martin Luther King's biography or his compelling letter from Birmingham Jail on April 16, 1963. While you are reading, notice any misfortunes the successful person had to overcome, especially those that attacked his or her self-esteem. Try to put yourself in his or her shoes and think about how you would have dealt with specific situations. Learn to continuously improve in every way possible. When you are following the success of others, try not to get carried away in just admiring them. Start to think of healthy self-esteem as something that you already have. You do have it; it may just be out of focus, or you may be out of touch with it. Picture yourself when reading or watching biographies as discovering a lost treasure—your own self-worth.

- *Make a list of your greatest talents.* If you draw a blank, ask someone close to you. A friend, family member, or significant other can help you start the list. Others will often see your good points, talents, and abilities more clearly than you see them yourself. Update your list on a regular basis and refer back to your list during challenging times. Your list will continuously mature, both in terms of meaning and length. Once you have compiled a list, consider each talent as a section of your new self-concept.

- *Stop procrastinating.* Most people procrastinate, and procrastination can hurt self-esteem a great deal. When you are not working toward goals, this can easily bring your self-esteem even lower. Getting tasks completed will give you a feeling of being "on top of things," which is very important to high self-esteem. Set goals and reward yourself for accomplishing each goal one step at a time.

- *Find a mentor.* A mentor is someone who will walk you through experiences that are new to you, but that he or she has already been through. True mentoring involves two people communicating well, one mostly teaching (mentor) and the other mostly learning (mentee). If you find someone who will work with you in this way, you've discovered an excellent method of learning. Remember that mentors are people who will help you be a better you. Once again, don't lose your identity in the process by adopting their habits. You need to find success in your own strengths while developing your weaknesses.

- *Avoid surface analysis of yourself and others.* Surface analysis means looking only at the apparent rather than underlying issues of life. You need to learn to be more understanding by focusing on the underling realties of all situations. There is a perfect cliché to exemplify this scenario: Don't judge a book by its cover. Learn to take chances because "a person who never made a mistake never tried anything new."

- *Use positive self-talk.* Positive self-talk is a popular method of building self-esteem by thinking and speaking positively about yourself. Using positive self-talk will become a self-fulfilling prophecy that means if you believe something strongly enough, it becomes a reality. Based on your beliefs and the actions that follow, you fulfill the prophecy or expectation you hold about your future. Promote positive self-talk, and you will instantly see the impact it will have on your life.

- *Don't forget the needs of others.* Competitiveness can keep people from allowing others to achieve the same things they are achieving. If you have this level of competitiveness, get rid of it. Be considerate of others and don't forget what goes around (whether good or bad) comes around. Give back to your community in every way possible.

- *Celebrate successes.* Don't forget to stop and celebrate each milestone. Celebrating success is mandatory and will rejuvenate a person's desire for reaching his or her end-goal. During your celebration, it is important to be able to reflect upon your accomplishments and plan your next milestone so you always have something to look forward to.

The Real World

When it is finally time to apply for your dream job, you need to have the correct balance of education, experience, and self-esteem that will help you shine throughout the screening and interviewing processes. At times, finding work can be a difficult task because of certain factors that are uncontrollable, such as the current declining economy with budget cuts in every organization. For example, one college professor explained,

> We currently have 1,200 students waitlisted at our college because we do not have the funds to open up more course sections. Many professors are being laid off as a result of the unfortunate budget cuts. I have been teaching at this college for over 20 years now and even my teaching course load has dropped from three courses each semester to only one. The college can't afford to pay their instructors.

During difficult economic times, those who are laid off from work usually end up going back to school to learn a new skill. The increase in demand for education and decrease in supply (seats available per classroom) have left every college and university in an absolute conundrum. With unemployment levels up, many find themselves applying for jobs that they are overqualified for in order to pay their bills. One college director explained the following,

> I have been hiring college instructors to teach at our college for the past three years. The minimum education requirement to teach at our college is for an applicant to have at least a master's degree. As a result of the economic crisis, I am finding that more applicants with higher levels of education are applying for work. In the past, out of 100 resumes that I would review, only five applicants would have a doctoral level degree and today, out of 100 resumes, only five applicants do not have a doctoral level degree. The reality is that those who only meet the minimum requirements do not stand a chance.

Finding work during difficult economic times is strenuous because of the unwanted competition and the limited amount of jobs. Knowing a lot of people (networking) and having the right connections (people with hiring authority) can be the key for survival during tough economical times. Many organizations have also been forced to lay off employees and distribute their work to the remaining employees. Those who are considered "valuable" or "efficient" usually survive many rounds of layoffs. One electrical engineer shared his tragic fate,

> I was an average worker in regards to my education level, productivity level, and popularity level at work. I was able to survive the first round of layoffs, which eliminated all of the sub-optimal employees, and then when the second round of layoffs hit, all of the mediocre performers were pink-slipped; I was included in that round. I was in a state of denial.

Being able to overcome obstacles is a necessity in life because life doesn't always go as planned. At the end of the day, it is important to be able to improvise and compromise.

The Educational Journey*

The educational journey teaches students more than just theoretical constructs and the application of theories. Students learn certain qualities that allow them to be better organizational and societal citizens. These qualities shape a society by manifesting a specific etiquette that has become the status quo for developed nations. The following unspoken qualities are "enhanced" or maybe even "acquired" by those who obtain an education.

- *Focus.* Students learn the importance of focus throughout school. Students focus during lectures, exams, and when doing homework. Being able to focus is important because the human mind goes into a mode of canceling out all external distractions, so an individual can complete a task or goal with precision. Mastering the art of focus is stressed in sports, martial arts, and other cognitive activities.

---

* Adapted from: *WCC Antioch Quarterly Newsletter*, Kaifi, B.A. (2010), 1(4), and also *Human Relations*, Lamberton, L., & Minor, L. (2010).

- *Respect.* Students learn the importance of respect throughout school. Students learn to respect their peers and teachers. Students learn that respect is something that is earned and not something that is expected. Having respect for others is a fundamental necessity to be able to function in a society with diverse people who have diverse views. Always remember that respect is a two-way street.

- *Responsibility and accountability.* Students learn the importance of responsibility and accountability throughout school. Students are responsible and accountable for their actions on a daily basis, which becomes a life-long practice. Being responsible and accountable are characteristics that are needed in all situations because those who are responsible and accountable are the ones who become successful.

- *Discipline.* Students learn the importance of discipline throughout school. Discipline allows a student to make the right choices when nobody is watching. Having self-discipline is a characteristic that can be developed and is a vital quality when having to complete projects or tasks. Those who do not have discipline are usually the ones who fall behind. Discipline is needed to fight off all temptations of a society.

- *Trust and being trusted.* Students learn the importance of trust throughout school. Teachers trust their students to make ethical decisions on a daily basis. It is important to be able to build a two-way trust relationship with your peers and to never break that trust. Being trusted takes time, but losing that trust can happen instantly. Trustworthiness is a quality that is both delicate and sincere.

Final Summary

This comprehensive book was meant for students and life-long learners who are seeking educational guidance. Many students waste valuable time by not doing their homework ahead of time and end up paying the price. Each chapter of this book was written for students in different stages of their educational journey. The interviews that were conducted with professionals from different fields illuminated the dedication that is needed to be academically successful. Throughout the book, tips and strategies were shared to help others in their endeavors. The wealth of information and knowledge compiled in this book should live on forever and should be a starting point for many important decisions.

Do not follow where the path may lead.
Go instead where there is no path and leave a trail.
Harold R. McClendon

If your actions inspire others to dream more,
learn more, do more and become more, you are a leader.
John Quincy Adams

The ultimate measure of a man is not where he stands in moments of comfort, but where he stands at times of challenge and controversy.
Dr. Martin Luther King, Jr.

BIBLIOGRAPHY

Adams, J. (1984). Transforming work. Alexandria, VA: Miles River Press.

Agarwal, S., & Mital, M. (2009). An exploratory study of Indian university students' use of social networking web sites: Implication for the workplace. Business Communication Quarterly, 72(1), pp. 105-110.

Ahiakpor, J. (1985). The success and failure of dependency theory: the experience in Ghana. International Organization, 39 (3), pp. 535-552.

Austin, R., Nolan, R., & O'Donnell, S. (2009). The technology manager's journey: An extended narrative approach to education technical leaders. Academy of Management Learning & Education, 8 (3), pp. 337-355.

Babcock, L. (2008). What happens when women don't ask? Negotiation, 11(96), pp. 1- 4.

Banner, D. K. (1995). Conflict resolution: A re-contextualization. Leadership and Organization Development Journal, 16 (1), pp. 2 - 4.

Beckman, D. & Menkhoff, L. (2008). Will women be women? Analyzing the gender difference among financial experts. Kyklos, 61(3), pp. 364-384.

Blank, I. (2008). Selecting employees based on emotional intelligence competencies: Reap rewards and minimize risk. Employee Relations Law Journal, 34(3), pp. 77- 85.

Bolman, L.G., & Deal, T.E. (2003). Reframing organizations (3rd ed.). San Francisco: Jossey-Bass.

Brown, A.L., Campione, J.C., & Dapy, J.D. (1981). Learning to learn: On training students to learn from texts. Educational Research, 10 (2), pp. 14-21.

Burka, J., & Yuen, L. (1983). Procrastination. Cambridge, MA: Perseus Books.

Cabrera, E. (2009). Fixing the leaky pipeline: Five ways to retain female talent. People and Strategy, 32(1), pp. 40- 45.

Cavico, F. & Mujtaba, B. G., (2008). Legal challenges for the global manager and Entrepreneur. Kendal Hunt Publishing Company. United States.

Cavico, F. J. & Mujtaba, B. G. (2009). Business ethics: The moral foundation of leadership, management, and entrepreneurship (2nd edition). Pearson Custom Publications. Boston, United States.

Chang, S.H., & Smith, R.A. (2008). Effectiveness of personal interaction in a learner centered paradigm distance education class based on student satisfaction. Journal of Research on Technology in Education, 40(4), pp. 407- 426.

Ciccarelli, S., & Meyer, G. (2006). Psychology. NJ: Pearson Prentice Hall.

Collier, V. (1989). How long: A synthesis of research on academic achievement in a second language. TESOL Quarterly, 23, pp. 509-531.

Conger, J. A., & Kanungo, R. N. (1998). Charismatic leadership in organizations. Thousand Oaks, CA: Sage.

Cook, R., Ley, K., Crawford, C., & Warner, A. (2009). Motivators and inhibitors for university faculty in distance and e-learning. British Journal of Educational Technology, 40 (1), pp. 149-163.

Cooper, T. (1998). The responsible administrator (4th ed.). San Francisco, CA: Jossey Bass.

Cornwall, J. (2009). Becoming a Classroom Facilitator - Entrepreneurship Education Newsletter. The Entrepreneurship Educator, February 09. Received on February 18, 2009 from: newsletter@planningshop.com.

Correia, A., & Davis, N. (2008). Intersecting communities of practice in distance education: the program team and the online course community. Journal of Distance Education, 29 (3), pp. 289- 306.

Dastoor, B., Roofe, E., and Mujtaba, B. (2005). Value Orientation of Jamaicans Compared to Students in the United States of America. International Business and   Economics Research Journal, 4(3), pp. 43-52.

De Maria, W. (2008). Cross cultural trespass: Assessing African anti-corruption capacity. International Journal of Cross Cultural Management, 8(3), pp. 317-341.

Denhardt, R. (1993). Theories of public organization. Belmont, CA: Wadsworth.

Deniz, M., Tras, Z., & Aydogan, D. (2009). An investigation of academic procrastination, locus of control, and emotional intelligence. Educational Science: Theory and Practice, 9 (2), pp. 623-632.

Desai, M., Hart, J., & Richards, T. (2008). E-learning: Paradigm shift in education. Education, 129(2), pp. 327-334.

Diaz-Rico, L.T. & Weed, K.Z. (2005). The cross-cultural, language, and academic development handbook: A complete K-12 reference guide. Boston, MA: Allyn-Bacon.

Dos Santos, T. (1970). The structure of dependence. American Economic Review, 60(2), pp. 231-236.

Eastmond, D. (1998). Adult learners and Internet-based distance education. New Directions for Adult and Continuing Education, 78, pp. 33-41.

Egbu, C. (1999). Skills, knowledge and competencies for managing construction refurbishment work. Construction Management and Economics, 17(1), pp. 29-43.

Ellis, J.K. & Fouts J.T. (1994). Research on school restructuring. Princeton Junction, NJ: Eye on Education, Inc.

Fortner, B. (2005). U.S. universities sign distance learning education contract with India. Civil Engineering, 75(11), p. 28.

Freeman, Y. & Freeman D. (2000). Closing the achievement gap. Thousand Oaks, CA: Heinemann.

Freire, P. (1999). Pedagogy of the oppressed. New York: Continuum.

Freire, P. (1993). Pedagogy of the city. New York, NY: Continuum.

Gardenswartz, L., Rowe, A., Digh, P., & Bennett, M. F. (2003). The global diversity desk reference: Managing an international workforce. San Francisco, CA: Pfeiffer.

Garmen, A., Burkhart, T., & Strong, J. (2006). Business knowledge and skills. Journal of Healthcare Management, 51(2), pp. 81-85.

Gerhart, B. (2008). Cross cultural management research: Assumptions, evidence, and suggested directions. International Journal of Cross Cultural Management, 8(3), pp. 259-274.

Gibson, S., Harris, M., & Colaric, S. (2008). Technology acceptance in an academic context: Faculty acceptance of online education. Journal of Education, 83(6), pp. 355-359.

Gladwell, M. (2002). The tipping point. New York: Little, Brown and Company.

Gladwell, M. (2008). Outliers: The story of success. New York: Little, Brown and Company.

Glesne, C. (2006). Becoming qualitative researchers: An introduction. Boston: Pearson/Allyn & Bacon.

Graham, S. (2008). Culturally proficient inquires: A lens for identifying and examining education gaps. San Francisco, CA: Crowin Press.

Hannum, W.H., Irvin, M.J., Lei, P., & Farmer, T.W. (2008). Effectiveness of using learner-centered principles on student retention in distance education courses in rural schools. Distance Education, 29 (3), pp. 211-229.

Harzing, A. (2006). Response styles in cross-national survey research: A 26-country study. International Journal of Cross Cultural Management, 6(2), pp. 243-266.

Henke, H. & Russum, J. (2000). Factors influencing attrition rates in a corporate distance education program. Education at a distance, 14 (11), Article 03. Retrieved July 25, 2001 from http://www.usdla.org/ED_magazine/illuminactive/ NOV00_Issue/ story03.htm

Herda, E.A. (1999). Research conversations and narrative: A critical hermeneutic orientation in participatory inquiry. Westport, CT: Praeger Publishers.

Himanshu, R. (2009). Gender differences: Ingratiation and leader member exchange quality. Singapore Management Review, 31(1), pp. 63-72.

Hofstede, G. (2001). Culture's consequences: Comparing values, behaviors, institutions, and organizations across nations (2nd ed.). Thousand Oaks, CA: Sage.

Hunter, M.C. (1987). Beyond reading, Dewey: What's next? A response to Gibboney. Educational Leadership, 44, pp. 51-54.

Ishii, S. & Bruneau, T. (1994). Silence and silences in cross-cultural perspective: Japan and the United States. In L. A. Samovar & R. E. Porter (Eds.), Intercultural communication: A reader (7th ed.) (pp.246-251). Belmont, CA: Wadsworth.

Jackson, T., Hill, S., Tamangani, Z., & Chipanbira, F. (2000). The management of people and organizations in South Africa and Zimbabwe: A cross-cultural study. Management Research News, 23(2), pp. 98-100.

Jackson, M.J., & Helms, M.M. (2008). Student perceptions of hybrid courses: Measuring and interpreting quality. Journal of Education for Business, 84(1), pp. 7-12.

Johnson, G.M., & Bratt, S.E. (2009). Technology education students: e-tutors for school children. British Journal of Educational Technology, 40(1), pp. 32-41.

Jones, G. R., & George, J. M. (2009). Contemporary management. New York: McGraw Hill.

Kaifi, B.A. (2008). The power of education in international economic development. Sitara Magazine, 1(5), pp. 16-17.

Kaifi, B.A. (2009). 21st century leadership in healthcare. Pages 90-100. Chapter Twelve in the Pharmaceutical Technician Laboratory Manual by Sandeep Bansal. Jones and Bartlett Publications, Boston, Massachusetts.

Kaifi, B.A. (2009). The Impact of 9/11 on Afghan-American Leaders. Bloomington, IN: Xlibris.

Kaifi, B.A., & Mujtaba, B.G. (2009). Workforce discrimination: An inquiry on the perspectives of Afghan-American Professionals. Journal of Business Studies Quarterly, 1(1), pp. 1-15.

Kaifi, B.A., Williams, A., & Mujtaba, B.G. (2009). Online college education for computer-savvy students: A study of perceptions and needs. Journal of College Teaching Methods and Styles, 6(10), pp. 1-15.

Kaifi, B.A. (2009). Online education. Antioch Quarterly Newsletter, 1(3), p. 2.

Kaifi, B.A. (2009). Understanding Procrastination. Antioch Quarterly Newsletter, 1(2), pp. 2-3.

Kaifi, B.A. (2009). Math SLO assessment: Case study in improvement. Newsletter of the WCC SLO Committee, 1(4), pp. 2-3.

Kaifi, B.A. (2010). Strategies for success. Antioch Quarterly Newsletter, 1(4), p. 2.

Kaifi, B.A. (2010). Math SLO assessment: Follow-up study on improvement. Newsletter of the WCC SLO Committee, 1(4), pp. 2-3.

Kaifi, B.A., Mujtaba, B.G., & Williams, A. (2010). The feasibility of distance education for cyber-savvy students. Journal of Quarterly Review and Distance Education, 10(4), pp. 347-350.

Kaifi, B.A. (2009). What color is your parachute? Journal of Applied Management and Entrepreneurship, 14(4), pp. 72-75.

Kaifi, B.A., and Mujtaba, B. G. (2010). Transformational leadership and the impact of socialization in the Afghan culture: a study of behavioral differences based on gender, age, and place of birth. *International Leadership Journal*, 2(2), 33-52.

Karadjova-Stoev, G., & Mujtaba, B. G. (2009). Strategic human resource management and global expansion lessons from the Euro Disney challenges in France. International Business and Economics Research Journal, 8(1), pp. 69-78.

Karahalios, M., & Mujtaba, G. B. (2006). Women, disabilities, technology, and the reconstruction of Afghanistan. Society of Afghan Engineers Journal, 3(1), pp. 38- 47.

Katz, R. L. (1955). Skills of an effective administrator. Harvard Business Review, 33 (1), pp. 33-42.

Kegan, R. (1994). In over our heads. Cambridge, MA: Harvard University Press.

Kirk, M. (2010). Straight A's—but still not ready for college. Oakland Tribune Newspaper article accessed February 17, 2010, p. A19.

Knouse, S.B. (2009). Targeted recruiting for diversity: Strategy, impression management, realistic expectations, and diversity climate. International Journal of Management, 26(3), pp. 347- 353.

Kotter, J.P. (1996). Leading change. Boston, MA: Harvard Business School Press.

Kouzes, J.M., & Posner, B.Z. (2003). Encouraging the heart. San Francisco: Jossey Bass.

Kreitner, R. (2007). Management (10th ed.). Boston, MA: Houghton Mifflin.

Lamberton, L.H., & Minor, L. (2010). Human Relations (4th ed.). Boston, MA: McGraw Hill.

Lantz, P. (2008). Gender and leadership in healthcare Administration: 21st century progress and challenges. Journal of Healthcare Management, 53(5), pp. 291- 301.

Lawrence-Lightfoot, S. (2000). Respect. Cambridge, MA: Perseus Books.

Leithwood, K., & Louis, K.S. (2004). Learning leadership project: How leadership influences student learning. New York: The Wallace Foundation.

Lopez-Fernandez, M., Martin-Alcazar, F., & Romero-Fernandez, P. (2009). Key factors in the access to managerial posts. Journal of General Management, 34(4), pp. 39- 50.

Loucks, S. F. & Zacchei, D. (1983). Applying our findings to today's innovation. Educational Leadership. 41, pp. 28-31.

Mandel, M. (2009). Economics: The basics. Boston, MA: McGraw-Hill.

McGrath, M.E., & McGrath, C.K. (2009). Decide better for college. Addison, TX: Motivation Publishing.

Marzano, R. (2005). School leadership that works. Alexandria, VA: Association for Supervision and Curriculum Development.

Mead, R. (2005). International management: Cross-cultural dimensions (3rd ed.). Malden, MA: Blackwell Business.

Menchaca, M.P. & Bekele, T.A. (2008). Learner and instructor identified success factors in distance education. Distance Education, 29 (3), pp. 231-252.

Morrison, A., & Glinow, M. (1995). Women and minorities in management. Chapter 28 in The Leader's Companion by J. Thomas Wren, pp. 168- 181. NY: The Free Press.

Mujtaba, B. G. (2008). Task and relationship orientation of Thai and American business students' based on cultural contexts. Research in Higher Education Journal, 1(1), pp. 38-57.

Mujtaba, B. G. (2008). Interpersonal change through the "Inside-Out-Approach": Exercising the freedom to choose our responses during conflict and stressful Situations. RU International Journal, 2(1), pp. 1-12.

Mujtaba, B. G. (2005). Faculty development practices in distance education for success with culturally diverse students. International Business and Economics Research Journal, 4(4), pp. 1-13.

Mujtaba, B. G., & McAtavey, J. (2006). Performance assessment and comparison of learning in international education: American versus Jamaican students' learning outcomes. The College Teaching Methods & Styles Journal, 2(3), pp. 33-43.

Mujtaba, B. G., & Mujtaba, L. (2004). Creating a healthy learning environment for student success in the classroom. The Internet TESL Journal. The article can be retrieved via the following URL link: http://iteslj.org/ or: http://iteslj.org/Articles/Mujtaba-Environment.html.

Mujtaba, B. G., & Mujtaba, L. (2004). Diversity awareness and management in adult education. Journal of College Teaching and Learning. 1(3), pp. 65-75.

Mujtaba, B. G., Preziosi, R., & Mujtaba, L. (2004). Adult learning, assessment, and the extraordinary teacher. Journal of College Teaching and Learning. 1(4), pp. 29-37.

Mujtaba, B. G., & Scharff, M. M. (2007). Earning a doctorate degree in the 21st century: Challenges and joys. ILEAD Academy Publications; Florida, USA.

Mujtaba, B. G. (2007). Cross cultural management and negotiation practices. ILEAD Academy Publications; Florida, United States.

Mumford, M.D., Zaccarro, S.J., Connelly, M.S., & Marks, M.A. (2000). Leadership skills: Conclusions and future directions. Leadership Quarterly, 11(1), pp. 155-170.

Munck, R. (1999). Dependency and imperialism in the new times: A Latin America perspective. The European Journal of Development Research, 11(1), pp. 56-74.

Munene, J. C., Schwartz, S. H., & Smith, P. B. (2000). Development in sub-Saharan Africa: Cultural influences and managers' decision behavior. Public Administration and Development, 20 (4), pp. 339-351.

Neely, L., Niemi, J. & Ehrhard, B. (1998). Classes going the distance so people don't have to: Instructional opportunities for adult learners. T.H.E. Journal, 26(4), p. 72.

Nieves, R.; Mujtaba, B. G.; Pellet, P.; and Cavico, F. J. (2006). Culture and Universal Professional Values in Global Organizations: Is there a Divergence or Convergence of Cultural Values? Journal of Diversity Management, 1(1), pp. 31-38.

Northouse, P.G. (2004). Leadership: Theory and practice (3rd ed.). London: Sage Publications.

Northouse, P. G. (2007). Leadership: Theory and practice (4th ed.). Thousand Oaks, CA: SAGE.

Northouse, P. G. (2010). Leadership: Theory and practice (5th edition). Los Angeles: Sage Publications.

Norton, P., & Hathaway, D. (2008). Exploring two teacher education online learning designs: A classroom of one or many? Journal of Research on Technology in Education, 40 (4), pp. 475- 495.

Notar, C., Herring, D., & Restauri, S. (2008). A web-based teaching aid for presenting the concepts of norm referenced and criterion referenced testing. Education, 129 (1), pp. 119-124.

Oyserman, D., Coon, H. M., & Kemmelmeier, M. (2002). Rethinking individualism and collectivism: Evaluation of theoretical assumptions and meta-analysis. Psychological Bulletin, 128(1), pp. 3-72.

Perraton, J. (2007). Evaluating Marxian contributions to development economies. Journal of Economic Methodology, 14(1), pp. 27-46.

Poole, D. (2000). Student participation in a discussion-oriented online course: A case study. Journal of Research on Computing in Education, 33 (2), pp. 162-77.

Postrel, S. (2009). Multitasking teams with variable complementarity: Challenges for capability management, Academy of Management Review, 34(2), pp. 273-296.

Pudlowski, E.M. (2009). Managing human resource cost in a declining economic environment. Benefits Quarterly, 25(4), pp. 37- 43.

Rahman, S., & Yang, L. (2009). Skill requirements for logistic managers in China: An empirical assessment. IIMB Management Review, 21(2), pp. 140-148.

Rainey, H. G. (2003). Understanding and managing pubic organizations (3rd ed). San Francisco, California: Jossey-Bass.

Reeves, P. (2004). Increasing organization capacity: A systems approach utilizing transformational and distributed leadership practices. Michigan, WI: Western Michigan University.

Reich, R. (2002). I'll be short: Essentials for a decent working society. Boston, MA: Beacon Press.

Richards, C. & Ridley, D. (1997). Factors affecting college students' persistence in online computer-managed instruction. College Student Journal, 31, pp. 490-495.

Robbins, S. & Coulter, M. (2005). Management (8th ed). NJ: Pearson.

Roblyer, M. (1999). Is choice important in distance learning? A study of student motives for taking Internet-based courses at the high school and community college levels. Journal of Research on Computing in Education, 32 (1), pp. 157-171.

Rossman, M. (2000). Andragogy and distance education: Together in the new millennium. New Horizons in Adult Education, 14 (1), 3-9. Retrieved from http://www.nova.edu/~aed/horizons/vol14n1.htm

Scarborough, J. (1998). The origins of cultural differences and their impact on management. Westport, CN: Quorum Books.

Schwartz, S. H. (1999). Cultural value differences: Some implications for work. Applied Psychology, 48(1), pp. 23-47.

Shin, M. & Lee, Y. (2009). Changing the landscape of teacher education via online teaching and learning. Techniques: Connecting Education & Careers, 83 (9), pp. 32-33.

Singham, M. (2003). The achievement gap: Myths and reality. Phi Delta Kappan, 84 (8), pp. 586 -591.

Smircich, L., & Stubbart, C. (1985). Strategic management in an enacted world. Academy of Management Review, 10, pp. 724-736.

Smith, R.O. (2008). The paradox of trust in online collaborative groups. Distance Education, 29 (3), pp. 325- 340.

Tatum, B. (1997). Why are the black kids sitting together in the cafeteria? NY: Basic Books.

Tensey, R. & Hyman, M. (1994). Dependency theory and the effects on advertising by foreign-based multinational corporations in Latin America. Journal of Advertising, 23(1), pp. 27-42.

Terry, N. (2001). Assessing enrollment and attrition rates for the online MBA. T.H.E. Journal, 28 (7), pp. 64-68.

Thomas, E., & Wingert, P. (2010). The key to saving American education. Newsweek article from March 15th 2010, pp. 24-33.

Tregarthen, T., & Rittenberg, L. (2000). Economics (2nd ed.). NY: Worth Publishers.

Tzabbar, D. (2009). When does scientist recruitment affect technological repositioning? Academy of Management Journal, 52 (5), pp. 873-896.

Velasco, A. (2002). Dependency theory. Foreign Policy, 133, pp. 44-46.

Voges, K.E., Tworoger, L.C., & Bendixen, M. (2009). The role of organizational template in radical change. The Journal of Applied Management and Entrepreneurship, 14(3), pp. 27- 48.

Wahlstedt, A., Pekkola, S., & Niemela, M. (2008). From e-learning space to e-learning place. British Journal of Educational Technology, 39 (6), pp. 1020 - 1030.

Weatherby, J.N., Arceneaux, C., Evans, E.B., Long, D., Reed, I., & Novika-Carter, O.D. (2009). The other world: Issues and Politics of the Developing world (8th ed). NY: Pearson.

Worrell, F. (2010). Straight A's—but still not ready for college. Oakland Tribune Newspaper article accessed February 17, 2010, p. A19.

Wren, J. (1995). The leader's companion: Insights in leadership through the ages. New York: The Free Press.

Wu, X., & He, J. (2009). Paradigm shifts in public administration: implications for teaching in professional training programs. Public Administration Education, 69, pp. 21-28.

Wyld, D. (2008). How do women fare when the promotion rules change? Academy of Management Perspectives, 22(4), pp. 83-85.

About the Author

Dr. Belal A. Kaifi completed his post-doctoral training in Business Administration with an emphasis in Management and Marketing at the University of Florida. He earned his doctoral degree in Organization and Leadership with an emphasis in Education from the University of San Francisco. He also earned a master's degree in Public Administration with an emphasis in Human Resources Management and a second master's degree in Business Administration, and a bachelor's degree in Business Administration with an emphasis in Management. Belal is academically qualified (AQ) to teach in the departments of Business Administration and Education. Belal has authored *"The Impact of 9/11 on Afghan-American Leaders"* and has published several articles in peer-reviewed academic journals both nationally and internationally. He has over ten years of combined experience in academia, including teaching at the undergraduate and graduate levels (both traditional classrooms and online), managing an educational department, consulting, and researching.

In 2005, Belal spent one month in Kabul, Afghanistan teaching English to high school students. He enjoys traveling and has spent time in Sweden, Dubai, Afghanistan, Canada, Mexico, and Germany.

INDEX